SAMURAI SIEGES

ALSO BY WILLIAM DE LANGE:

Samurai Battles
The Siege of Ōsaka Castle
An Encyclopedia of Japanese Castles
A Fool's Journey
A Fool's Return
Musashi: Fact & Fiction
The Real Musashi, I, II, III
Famous Samurai, I, II, III
The Remarkable History of the Yaggyū Clan
A Dictionary of Japanese Onomatopeoia
A Dictionary of Japanese Proverbs
A Dictionary of Japanese Idioms
A History of Japanese Journalism
The Namamugi Incident
Japanese Scrolls
Pars Japonica
Iaido

PUBLISHED IN THE SAME SERIES:

Eiko Ozaki, *Warriors of Old Japan*

SAMURAI SIEGES

THE LONG ROAD TO UNIFICATION

WILLIAM DE LANGE

For more on books by William de Lange visit:
www.williamdelange.com

First edition, 2023

Published by TOYO Press
Visit us at: **www.toyopress.com**

ISBN 978-94-92722-430

CONTENTS

SHIGISAN

It is the year 1577. Oda Nobunaga, the upstart warlord from a small warrior clan in the southern part of Owari Province, has presided over a series of successful battles, beginning with his stunning victory over Imagawa Yoshimoto in the Battle of Okehazama in 1560. By now, the central provinces of Owari, Mino, and Ōmi are all under his control. In Mino, just north along the Nakasendō where it approaches the capital of Kyoto, he has built himself a new stronghold atop Mt. Azuchi. All those who set eyes on his magnificent castle cannot but fail to be impressed. One man to visit Azuchi Castle is the Jesuit missionary Luis Frois:

> Nobunaga built this palace, which in terms of strength, wealth, and grandeur, may be compared to the greatest buildings in Europe. Its massive surrounding walls are over 20 m in height, and in some places even higher. Inside are many exquisite buildings, all decorated with gold, and so well crafted that they seem the height of human elegance. At its center is a kind of keep they call a *tenshū*, which has a far more noble and splendid appearance than our keeps. It has seven floors, all of which, both on the inside, and on the outside, have been beautifully fashioned—inside the walls are decorated with designs in gold and different colors; outside, each of the stories is likewise painted in various

colors. Some are painted white with black varnished windows in Japanese style; others are painted red and blue, while the top one is entirely gilded.

Azuchi Castle is a veritable symbol of Nobunaga's power, a power he is intent on expanding, for large parts of Japan are still not under his control—both western and northern Japan are still cut up between a vast number of warlords fighting each other for bits of territory.

One such warlord is Matsunaga Hisahide. Hisahide is a formidable rival. With the help of the Miyoshi, he has brought the province of Yamato under his control, driving out the powerful Tsutsui and establishing two strongholds: Shigisan Castle on the border with Kawachi, and Tamonyama Castle on Nara's northern outskirts. Hisahide governs his newly conquered territories with an iron fist, punishing all opposition with unspeakable acts of barbarity. As on the occasion when one of his vassals, Ido Yoshihiro, who soon tires of Hisahide's despotic rule, rises in revolt and joins the Tsutsui. In doing so he seals the fate of his daughter, who is held captive at Tamonyama Castle. On Hisahide's direct orders, she is dragged out of her confinement and beheaded. Her head is impaled on a long pole and put out on display at the castle's main gate.

Azuchi Castle at the height of its glory

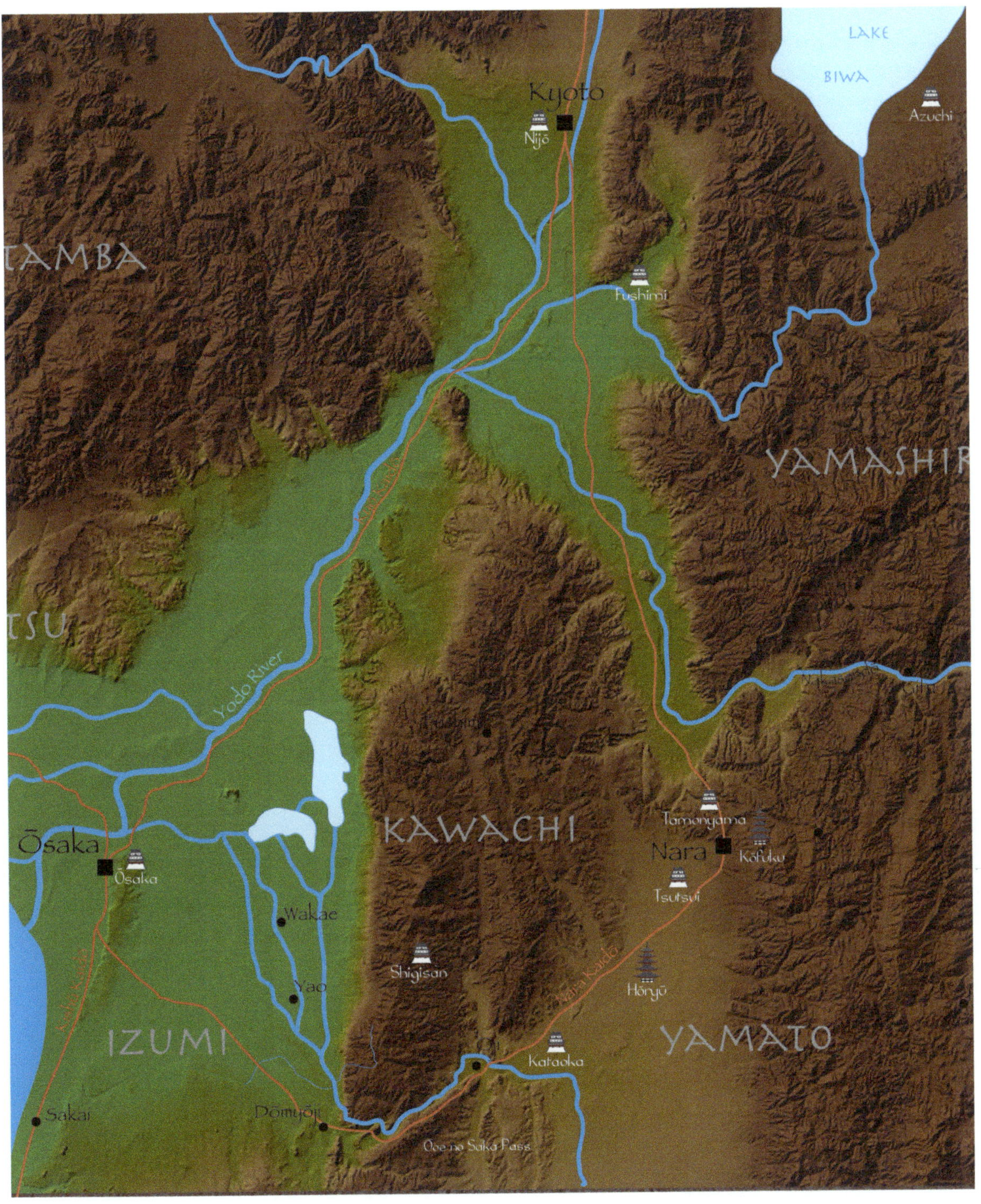
LAKE
BIWA
Azuchi
Kyoto
Nijō
TAMBA
Fushimi
YAMASHIR
TSU
Yodo River
KAWACHI
Tamonyama
Nara
Kōfuku
Ōsaka
Ōsaka
Tsutsui
Wakae
Shigisan
Hōryū
Nara Kaidō
Yao
Kishū Kaidō
IZUMI
YAMATO
Kataoka
Sakai
Dōmyōji
Oce no Saka Pass

Matsunaga Hisahide was born in 1508 as the son of a Sakai merchant. He rose to prominence by becoming the private secretary to Miyoshi Chōkei, a warlord from Shikoku who led his clan in a successful campaign to bring the provinces around the capital under his control. It was largely with the help of the Miyoshi that, during the 1540s, he launched a successful campaign to bring Yamato Province under Miyoshi control. It was a campaign during which he repeatedly displayed great tactical genius, and a campaign that was crowned, in 1565, with the fall of Tsutsui Castle and the expulsion of Hisahide's greatest rivals, the Tsutsui. By then, Miyoshi Chōkei had passed away following a short illness. His death was preceded by the mysterious death of his son and heir, Yoshioki, leaving Hisahide in effective control of Yamato Province, a control he strengthened by coercing most of the province's remaining clans into submission.

Hisahide's reign was marked by violence, treachery, and cruelty. And while some of it served a strategic purpose (to bind people to him in loyalty), much of it was gratuitous. Indeed, Hisahide seems to have taken great pleasure in seeing people suffer, turning his genius to new ways of inflicting pain, not only on his enemies but also on his subjects. One of his favorite methods of torturing peasants who had failed to raise enough in taxes was the so-called *minomushi-odori* or the 'dance of the raincoat bug,' in which he would have the hapless victim put on a straw raincoat and had his men set it alight.

Like many despots, Hisahide was also a deeply superstitious man. One frequent guest at Tamonyama Castle was the magician Kashin Koji. It is said that on one such occasion, late at night, Hisahide challenged the magician saying, 'Not once have I felt fear in combat, let's see if you can frighten me!' At this, the magician had all the candles in the room extinguished and cast his spell. And, lo and behold, before the warlord rose an apparition of his deceased wife while bursts of lightning outside lit up the paper windows. When the apparition finally dissolved, the warlord sat trembling in a corner and his face was as white as paper.

On a larger political scale, too, Hisahide evinces a remarkable lack of moral scruples. The tone of this career is set when, in 1563, he poisons the son of his benefactor and ally, Miyoshi Chōkei. It is copied by his son, Hisamichi, who, on 17 June 1565, assassinates *Shōgun* Ashikaga Yoshiteru at his palace along Kyoto's Nijō Avenue. Not even the Buddhist church is safe from Hisahide's will to power. When, on the evening of 10 November 1567, Tamonyama Castle is threatened by a Miyoshi-Tsutsui alliance encamped on the grounds of Nara's Daibutsuden, he orders his troops to open fire on the historic building. Before long fire spreads from the outbuildings to the main hall. When the sun rises over the smoking embers the next day, the roof of the building has collapsed and the upper torso of the giant bronze Buddha statue inside has melted away.

Nobunaga is not particularly troubled by Hisahide's penchant for violence. He, too, is capable of inflicting incredible suffering on those who oppose him. He, after all, has risen to prominence by assassinating two men: his cousin, Nobutomo, and his younger brother, Nobuyuki. And while he hasn't dared lay his hands on Yoshiteru's successor, Yoshiaki (probably because he is his protege), he does send him into exile when he conspires against him in 1573. Nor does he flinch from attacking the Buddhist church, most notably so in 1571, when he orders his men to set fire to the temples atop Mt. Hiei and slaughter all who escape the terrible flames.

Nobunaga, then, initially recognizes Hisahide's governorship over Yamato. Yet he soon comes to regret it, for, In Nobunaga's eyes, Hisahide displays one unforgivable sin: he is a fickle ally. Before long, word reaches Nobunaga that the former merchant is forming secret alliances with his most powerful enemies. With Takeda Shingen, for instance. In 1572, they intend to drive Nobunaga from Kyoto, a plan that fails when Shingen suddenly passes away the next year while returning home from his victorious battle against Tokugawa Ieyasu at Mikatagahara. To chastise Hisahide, Nobunaga sends his general Sakuma Nobumori into Yamato. Following a successful clash with Miyoshi forces, Nobumori marches on Tamonyama Castle, and after a short siege, forces Hisahide to surrender the castle.

Nobunaga pardons Hisahide. Many of his close retainers wonder why? But in his heart of hearts, Nobunaga knows all too well. Though in public he might look down on the Yamato warlord, in secret he admires him, for in some fields the merchant is his superior. As in the field of *cha nu yū*, for instance, the art of making tea, an art in which Nobunaga has invested much time and money to gain a name for himself among Sakai's and Kyoto's upper echelons. He has become a diligent student of the tea master Imai Sōkyū (1520–93). An arms dealer by trade and a member of Sakai's city council, Sōkyū's famed tea ceremonies form the lubricant in his many dealings with fellow merchants and customers, most of whom are powerful warlords equally obsessed with the art of tea. And one of the frequent guests at Sōkyū's tea parties is Matsunaga Hisahide.

Hisahide has been quick to use his standing in the world of merchants and turn it to his political advantage. In 1568, when Nobunaga marched on the capital and installed his protege, Ashikaga Yoshiaki, as the 15th *shōgun* of the Muromachi *bakufu*, Hisahide had been one of the first to publicly acknowledge Nobunaga's ascendancy. Shortly afterward, during an audience with Nobunaga in Kyoto, he presented him with the legendary Tsukumokaminasu, a tea caddy so priceless that it was said to have attained a *kami* spirit. Not a man averse to flattery, Nobunaga was quickly won over by Hisahide's charm. He even returned the warlord's flattery. During a tea ceremony to which he invited Hisahide not long afterward, he served him a bowl of tea with the words: 'I will treasure the tea caddy you gave me until the end of my days.'

This time, too, Hisahide is quick to make amends. Visiting Nobunaga at Gifu Castle the year after the loss of Tamonyama Castle, he renews his pledges of allegiance and showers the warlord with yet more costly gifts. He also offers up his two grandsons to serve as hostages against his loyalty. And again Nobunaga is assuaged, for there is another reason why he looks up to Hisahide: his genius in the field of castle architecture. At this point, Nobunaga is still working on his new stronghold atop Mt. Azuchi. He wants it to be the most opulent, the most modern stronghold in the realm. And one of the examples he looks toward is Hisahide's stronghold on Nara's outskirts. It is no secret that Tamonyama Castle is one of the most modern and innovative strongholds in the realm. Through different channels, he has learned of Tamonyama Castle's splendor—how it makes most of Japan's existing strongholds look like primitive hovels. It is for this reason that, when he dispatched Sakuma Nobumori into Yamato, he made sure to instruct him to 'seize Tamonyama Castle but spare it.' Four months later, on 18 April, Nobunaga too goes down to Nara. Having first paid a visit to the Tōdai Temple's Shōsō Monastery to take some cuttings from a yew tree growing on its grounds, he enters Tamonyama Castle to conduct an inspection. During that inspection, he notes how Hisahide has improved on the *hashiri-yagura*, the 'running turrets' of traditional castles, and replaced them with elongated structures with tiled roofs and plastered walls beset with loopholes that sit atop the castle walls and cover their entire circumference. Tamonyama Castle's structures are so new and innovative that they are already known as *tamon-yagura*. To duplicate these structures, Nobunaga hires artisans from Yamato who have worked on Tamonyama Castle to do the same at his stronghold of Azuchi Castle.

Needless to say, Nobunaga has been prudent enough to also take away Hisahide's governorship over Yamato Province, leaving him only his stronghold of Shigisan Castle on its western border. The governorship is bestowed on Ban Naomasa, a close retainer who goes on to render distinguished services in the battle of Nagashino as *teppō bugyō*. It is in the same capacity that Naomasa takes part in Nobunaga's campaign against the fanatic Ikkō sectarians ensconced at the Ishiyama Hongan-*ji*, a sprawling web of fortified temples and monasteries on a cluster of islands at the mouth of the Yodo River. When, four years later, on 26 June 1576, Naomasa is killed in action, the governorship of Yamato goes to Tsutsui Junkei, whose clan controlled much of Yamato before Hisahide arrived on the scene.

Hisahide is dismayed. He has spent most of the previous decade doing battle with Junkei, only to find that the latter has now been given the very governorship that has been taken away from him. Worse still, that same summer, Nobunaga orders his deputy (*shoshidai*) in Kyoto, Murai Sadakatsu, to oversee the complete destruction of Tamonyama Castle. Some of its structures are to be used to fortify Ashikaga Yoshiaki's palace along the Nijō avenue in Kyoto. By the summer of 1577, all that remains of the once so magnificent stronghold are its formidable stone walls. But then, on 28 October of that same year, while encamped at Tennōji, doing battle together with his son,

Hisamichi, against the Ikkō sectarians on behalf of Nobunaga, word reaches Hisahide that even his castle's stone walls are being demolished. What is worst is that they are being used for a stronghold arising just west of Nara: Kōriyama Castle, the new headquarters of none other than Tsutsui Junkei. For almost a year Hisahide has managed to suppress his pent-up anger, but this is the last straw. Flying into an uncontrollable rage, he orders his men to set fire to their encampment and to return to his stronghold of Shigisan Castle, which is only fifteen miles east up Mt. Shigi from where they are encamped. At that point, he is leading an army of some three hundred mounted warriors and eight thousand men on foot. And it is with this formidable force that he entrenches himself in his stronghold atop the mountain.

Not a man easily flustered, Nobunaga is nevertheless concerned. So much so that he dispatches Matsui Yūkan, the magistrate of Sakai and a fellow tea aficionado, toward Shigisan Castle to sound the warlord out. His message to Hisahide, according to the *Oda gunki*, is straightforward: 'Be frank and explain what exactly it is you have in mind. Once you have explained yourself, I am sure I will be able to overlook this matter.' Yet while Hisahide receives his guest in good grace and they enjoy some tea together, he refuses to budge. Moreover, soon word reaches Nobunaga that Hisahide has not just withdrawn from his campaign against the Ishiyama Hongan-*ji* but is actively conspiring against him—that he has sent word to Kōsa, the spiritual leader of the Ikkō sectarians, as well as the northern warlord, Uesugi Kenshin. As if to confirm the rumor, it is followed by the news, late in October that year, that Ikkō sectarians have launched attacks against his general Shibata Katsuie in Kaga, seemingly in an effort to aid Kenshin, who is readying some twenty-thousand men farther northward to march on the capital.

This time Nobunaga has had enough. From his headquarters of Azuchi Castle, he orders his senior general Akechi Mitsuhide to reduce Shigisan Castle. To achieve this, Mitsuhide is to join forces with Tsutsui Junkei and Hosokawa Fujitaka. Their combined strength amounts to some twenty thousand men. It is no excessive luxury. Shigisan Castle is a formidable stronghold. Sitting high atop Mt. Shigi, it boasts some of the best natural defenses a *yamashiro* or 'mountaintop castle' can offer. Mt. Shigi also isn't an isolated mountain that can be encircled. It is part of a long mountain range that de-

Tsutsui Junkei (1549–84) was born as the son of Tsutsui Junshō, a man who spent much of his life strengthening his clan's power base in Yamato. With Junshō's death, in 1550, followed by that of his brother and successor, Junsei, in exile at Sakai, the leadership of the Tsutsui clan finally evolves to Junkei.

By that time, the plight of the Tsutsui clan was already dire. They had lost their main seat of Tsutsui Castle to Matsunaga Hisahide and had gradually been driven out of their territories, all the way to Fuse Castle in Katsuragi, a hamlet on Yamato's western border. It was from there that the young Junkei launched a campaign to topple Hisahide. His first priority was to regain his family stronghold of Tsutsui Castle, and it was here—with the help of Hisahide's former allies, the Miyoshi—that the bold seventeen-year-old warrior achieved his first victory. On June 25, 1566, following a siege of several weeks, he evicted Hisahide's forces from the castle, gaining his first important foothold in Yamato.

Over the following decade, Junkei's forces repeatedly clashed with those of Hisahide, most dramatically so during their standoff on the grounds of Nara's Daibutsuden, which resulted in the historic building's partial destruction. It was a serious blow to Junkei's reputation, who professes to be a devout Buddhist and whose clan had a long and deep connection to Nara's Kōfuku Temple.

Junkei's ambition to restore the fortunes of the Tsutsui in Yamato received a powerful boost in 1571 when, through the offices of Akechi Mitsuhide, he became a direct ally of Oda Nobunaga. Four years later, so as to cement the new alliance between the Oda and the Tsutsui, he married one of Nobunaga's daughters. One year later, on 6 June 1576, Nobunaga officially recognized Junkei as the new governor of Yamato Province.

marcates the border between Yamato and Kawachi provinces. Countless hidden roads and paths through these mountains provide the castle's defenders with ample opportunity to resupply the stronghold with arms and provisions. Moreover, the main road of access up to the mountain, which is from the eastern Yamato plain, is guarded by Kataoka Castle, which is under the control of Ebina Katsumasa, one of Hisahide's close vassals. Once the seat of the local Kataoka clan, the small stronghold had been the first to fall when Hisahide launched his invasion of Yamato and now serves as a *shijō*, a 'satellite castle' to Hisahide's *honjō* or main castle of Shigisan.

Mitsuhide, Junkei, and Fujitaka set up camp on the grounds of the Hōryū Temple. From there it is just three miles southwest to Kataoka Castle. On 10 November 1577, they cross the Yamato River and launch an attack on the stronghold with a force of five thousand men. That same evening, the Buddhist monk Eishun, the abbot of the nearby Tamon Monastery, records in his diary, the *Tamon-in nikki*, that 'Today, they have attacked Kataoka Castle and some seventy Ebina men were cruelly slaughtered.' Less than a decade earlier, on 24 April 1569, Eishun had recorded in his diary how Matsunaga Hisahide's forces, too, had attacked the castle. Back then, it took Hisahide nine days to reduce the stronghold. This time around, the castle's defenders surrender within nine hours.

Nobunaga, who is following events closely back at Azuchi Castle, is pleased with this early progress and awards some of his warriors who have performed particularly well with letters of praise. Among them are two young warriors: Hosokawa Tadaoki, who is fourteen, and his brother Okimoto, who is only eleven. They were part of a spearhead unit and are the day's *ichiban-nori*, 'the first to breach the castle's defenses.'

For a moment Nobunaga's delight is dampened by the news that, up north, his general Shibata Katsuie, who has engaged with Uesugi Kenshin's forces at Tedorigawa, has been routed and has lost almost a thousand men. But he relaxes when he hears that, instead of marching on the capital, Kenshin retreats to his home province of Echigo. Exactly why he would want to miss such an opportunity to press his advantage is unclear to Nobunaga. Perhaps it is the approach of winter—when thick snowdrifts threaten to block the mountain passes—that keeps him from marching on the capital. There are also rumors

SHIGISAN

A young Hosokawa Okimoto and Oda Nobunaga's letter of praise (inset)

that Kenshin has his eyes set on the Kantō region and might instead move against the Hōjō at Odawara Castle. What is clear to Nobunaga is that he now has both hands free to tackle Hisahide at Shigisan Castle. And thus he orders all his forces deployed in Kaga to march down to Yamato and join those under the command of Mitsuhide, Junkei, and Fujitaka. Overall command is assumed by Nobunaga's oldest son Nobutada. The vanguard is led by Akechi Mitsuhide, while Hashiba (Toyotomi) Hideyoshi is to coordinate the actions of his remaining generals. Together they command a force of some forty thousand men, five times that of those defending the stronghold.

On 13 November, flames erupt from the Chōgonshi Temple. For nigh-on ten centuries, the temple has graced the western slope of Mt. Shigi, guarding the *Shigisan engi*, the ancient picture scrolls of the *Legend of Mount Shigi*, which recount the Three Miracles performed by the monk Myōren when, during the 10th century, he lived atop the mountain to worship the Buddha. It is

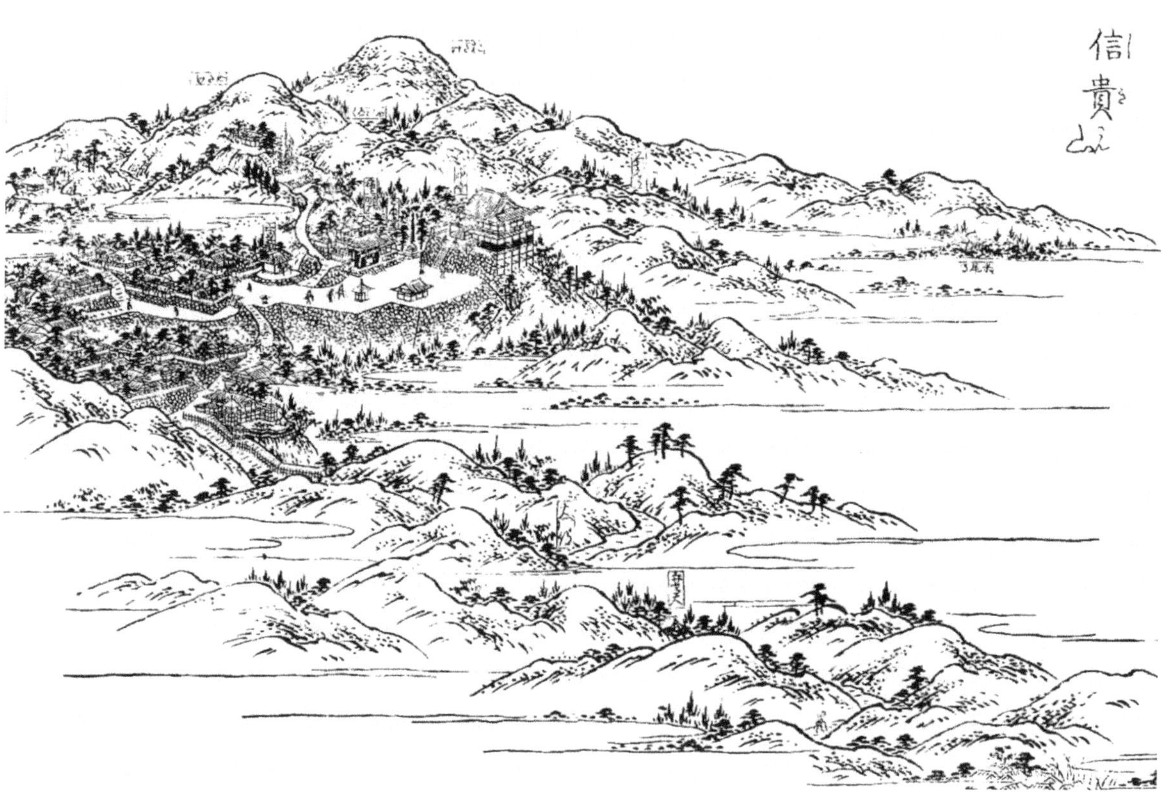

The Chōgonshi Temple

not clear who started the fire, but within hours the Bishamon-*dō*, the temple's main hall, is reduced to ashes. It is seen by many as a dark omen of the fate that awaits Shigisan Castle higher up the mountain.

The first major assault comes on the next day, 14 November, when Nobutada orders his entire army to storm the mountain. Wave upon wave of warriors hurl themselves at the castle, but each wave breaks on the stronghold's formidable defenses. During the two decades that it has been under his control, Hisahide has turned the castle into a veritable fortress. Each and every terrace on the mountain's irregular slopes has been turned into *kuruwa*, small baileys protected by raised parapets with loopholes. In total, there are a staggering one hundred and ten such *kuruwa*. Like flights of stairs, they ascend toward the top of the mountain, each *kuruwa* separated from the lower-lying one by so-called *hori-kiri*, deep dry moats that cut across the ridges to impede any further ascent. The mountain's natural ridges provide for six of these serrated flights of stairs, each, in turn, set off from the other by deep gorges that run from the foot to the top of the mountain. The stronghold's inner citadel, mounted at the mountain's crest like a veritable crown jewel, is flanked on the east by a second and third bailey. Three narrow roads provide access to the inner citadel, two from the east and one from the west, the main one passing the Chōgonshi Temple, but all three of them run a zigzag gauntlet up the heavily defended flights of stairs.

It is down the main road along the temple that, that same day, one of Hisahide's commanders, Handa Mototsugu, leads some two hundred men in a sortie against the enemy, killing and wounding almost the same number of Mitsuhide's spearhead of elite warriors. By the end of the day, hundreds of Nobutada's men are dead and many more are incapacitated by grave wounds. Nobunaga is so outraged by this setback, that he orders Hisahide's two grandsons to be executed. Even Nobunaga's close retainer, Ōta Gyūichi, is moved to tears when he records the demise of the boys in the *Shinchō kōki*, Nobunaga's official history:

> The two boys were loaded onto a cart at a crossroad along Kyoto's Ichijō avenue and brought to the capital's execution grounds at Rokujōgawara. There, the capital's populace, high and low, had already

> gathered to witness the spectacle. Both boys, without any change in color in their countenance, calmly turned to the west, and joining their small hands together, raised their voices to offer a prayer up to the Buddha. Then they fell silent as the swords came down on their frail necks. And all who witnessed this pitiable scene were moved to the core of their being, and all who heard their frail voices break were moved to tears.

Nobunaga's cruel act does not inspire Hisahide to show any contrition. This is even more true for the boys' father, Hisamichi, who vows to avenge their cruel end a thousand times. When he and his father withdrew their forces from Tennōji, he had initially returned to his headquarters of Yanagimoto Castle, just south of Nara. But now, hearing that both his sons are dead, and he is left without an heir, he abandons his stronghold and leads all of his men in an unanticipated and withering attack on the rear of the gathered forces. They are so much taken by surprise that Hisamichi and his men are able to break the cordon and join his father atop the mountain.

The first day of the siege has seen the Matsunaga victorious. But Hisahide knows that he and his men are fighting a losing battle. They are outnumbered five to one; soon his men will be depleted in such numbers that it will be impossible to hold the fortress. They need reinforcements, and they need them fast. With Uesugi Kenshin in retreat up north, his only hope is Kōsa, the abbot of the Ishiyama Hongan-*ji*. Enlisting his help, however, is a tall order. Up until only a few weeks ago, he and his son had been encamped at Tennōji fighting Kōsa's Ikkō sectarians along with Nobunaga's allies. To now persuade Kōsa to come to their aid requires skill and persuasion. Yet he has a man who seems cut for the job: Mori Yoshihisa. Though Yoshihisa once was a retainer of the Tsutsui, after the fall of Tsutsui Castle, he has spent several years as a *rōnin*, fighting for anyone who hired him. Along with many other *rōnin*, he joined the sectarians at the Ishiyama Hongan-*ji*, who are always in need of men and, with their wide network of supporters, have the money to pay them. More than a year he fought alongside the sectarians but, homesick for his native Yamato, he had seized the opportunity to return home when Hisahide began to hire warriors to man Tamonyama Castle.

Setting out from Shigisan on 15 November, Mori Yoshihisa returns two days later. With him are some two-hundred *teppō ashigaru*, all of them professing to also be former *rōnin* who had joined the sectarians in search of employment. True, it is only a drop in the ocean, but Yoshihisa assures his master that more help is on the way. The powerful Mōri from western Honshu, who are allied to the sectarians, are eager to frustrate Nobunaga in any way possible and have pledged more reinforcements. They are already on their way and are bound to arrive in a matter of days. Hisahide is delighted with Yoshihisa's mission and, by way of reward, puts him and his men in charge of the defense of the castle's third bailey. It is an important appointment as the third bailey forms the last major barrier to the castle's inner citadel.

Hostilities resume in full force the next day, November 18, when Oda Nobutada's forces again seek to reach the castle's inner citadel. Ferocious fighting continues throughout the day and night until, at dawn the next morning, Tsutsui Junkei implores Nobutada to let him lead the vanguard: Hisahide is his sworn enemy and he is sure his men are eager to wreak revenge for the suffering Hisahide has caused them and their kindred. The request is granted and by noon Junkei and his men have managed to push beyond the Chōgonshi Temple halfway up the mountain. There, they continue to meet stiff resistance, and when one of Hisahide's commanders again makes a sortie, the Tsutsui men are forced to retreat.

It is at this juncture, when all hangs in the balance, that Mori Yoshihisa's *teppō ashigaru* at the castle's third bailey open fire, not toward the enemy but toward the castle's second bailey and inner citadel. Yoshihisa has switched sides. Unbeknown to Hisahide, Yoshihisa never visited the Ishiyama Hongan-*ji*. No sooner did he descend from Mt. Shigi, than he headed for the camp of Matsukura Shigenobu, a Tsutsui retainer with whom he once shared a seat on Junkei's board of elders. It is Shigenobu who has furnished him with the two-hundred *teppō ashigaru*, along with a reward of thirty *ryō* in exchange for his defection. Were he to turn the battle in their favor, he has been told, he will be received back into the Tsutsui fold.

Yoshihisa's return to his place on Junkei's board of elders seems secure, for soon several of the structures within the castle's second bailey are enveloped in flames. Before long, the flames, fanned by a strong easterly wind

Hisahide's last moments

up the mountain, leap up toward the inner citadel, setting fire to the castle's magnificent four-story main keep, a keep that has been the model for the keep of Nobunaga's stronghold of Azuchi Castle.

Inside the keep, where Hisahide is hauled up with the remainder of his entourage, the realization sinks in that all is lost. From one of the keep's trellised windows, he watches on as his son, who has been leading the defense of the inner citadel, hurls himself from its steep walls into the flames below. All is lost. But Hisahide is not about to let Nobunaga put his head on display at the capital's entrance. If he is to depart this life, he is going to do so in style. Nor is he going to let Nobunaga lay his hands on his most prized tea utensil: the Hiragumo-*gama*, a cast-iron tea kettle that bears a remarkable resemblance to an indigenous spider. Filling the kettle up with gunpowder he prepares himself for the end, but not before he has called in his personal physician to have his final treatment of moxibustion to treat the palsy from which he suffers. The *Bizen rōjin monogatari* is one of the few records to describe the despot's last moments in vivid detail. As his physician places a small cone of burning moxa on the crown of the Hisahide's head, one of his retainers openly wonders, 'My lord, to what aim can such treatment be at such an hour?' Hisahide burst out laughing and replies:

Hisamichi hurls himself to his death

芳年武者无類
弾正忠松永久秀
大蘇芳年
彫工宗岡

> It might indeed seem odd to some. But the idea of losing control over my five limbs while I am about to meet my end truly fills me with terror. Were that to happen, all the military prowess I have displayed hitherto will be reduced to naught. It will have meant nothing. By thus staving off the symptoms of my affliction, I will be able to meet my end in comfort!

Then, having seen to it that all his kin have been put to death, he takes up the cast-iron kettle and retreats to the top of the castle's keep. There he places the Hirakumo-*gama* in front of him and detonates it. The blast is strong enough to destroy the keep's upper story.

The next day, the cinders having cooled down by a drizzling rain, one of Nobutada's men who is sifting through the rubble recovers Hisahide's head, the scar of moxibustion still visible on its crown. The head is sent to Azuchi Castle for Nobunaga's inspection. The remains of Hisahide's torso, too, are recovered. They are interred at what remains of the Daruma Temple. For more than three centuries, the temple had graced a hill in a curve of the Yamato River where it bends south and away from Mt. Shigi, only to be sacked and burned when Hisahide launched his invasion into Yamato. Presiding over the modest ceremony is Tsutsui Junkei, the man who has fought the tea merchant turned warlord for most of his adult life.

By the Japanese lunisolar calendar, Hisahide's last stronghold has fallen on the tenth day of the tenth month. A decade earlier, equally on the tenth day of the tenth month, Hisahide burned down Nara's ancient Daibutsuden. The point is not lost on Nobunaga's chronicler, Ōta Gyūichi, who ends his account of the castle's fall with the wry observation that:

> Nara's Daibutsuden, too, went up in flames on the tenth day of the tenth month. And it was this very same Hisahide who reduced it to ashes without good reason, and along with it the entire temple complex known throughout the realm. Thus it was heaven's retribution when Lord Oda Nobutada pressed home the attack on Shigisan Castle, a mountain so high that not even birds and beasts can find a foothold.

KŌZUKI

Though Matsunaga Hisahide and his son are now out of the way, Nobunaga still faces a monumental task in his aim to pacify the country. There are many powerful clans that oppose his ascendancy with all their might. Some of the most powerful among them are the Hōjō in the north and the Mōri in the west. And it is with the latter that he now wants to settle scores, and not only because his former protege Ashikaga Yoshiaki has sought refuge with the Mōri. Led by the wily Mōri Terumoto, the influence of the Mōri in western Japan is unsurpassed. Controlling a vast fleet of warships, they have been a constant menace in his campaign against the Ishiyama Hongan-*ji*. It has taken him already the better part of a decade to try and subdue the sprawling stronghold. If it wasn't for the Mōri, who supply the sectarians over water with arms and provisions, he would have achieved the same in less than a year.

Thus it is that, in the summer of the previous year, he has discussed with his generals his plan for his Chūgoku-*zeme*, the 'campaign to subdue the Chūgoku region,' the part of Honshū that lies west of the capital. It is vital that he move quickly. Already, the Mōri are moving eastward in a bid to seize the capital: the crown jewel. They are doing so along the Sanyōdō, the ancient highroad skirting the Inland Sea, and along the Sanindō, the highroad skirting the Sea of Japan. By now they have crossed the western border

of the province of Harima, where they set up a power base at Kōzuki Castle to serve as a springboard for their final push toward the capital.

Nobunaga's campaign seriously kicks into action early in November 1577, when his right-hand general Hashiba Hideyoshi marches into Harima and sets up his new headquarters at Himeji Castle, a small stronghold at the crest of Mt. Hime. It is an old castle, built in 1346 at the site where once stood the Shōmyō Temple. The temple was not demolished but carefully dismantled and now stands at the foot of Mt. Hime. The present lord of Himeji Castle is Kuroda Yoshitaka, a local chieftain who has declared himself on Nobunaga's side early on and has already rendered valuable service in Nobunaga's campaign to subdue central Japan. The two men get off to a good start and, with an intimate knowledge of the terrain and local power politics, Yoshitaka soon becomes one of Hideyoshi's most senior advisers during the Chūgoku campaign. Next to Kōzuki Castle, he informs

Hideyoshi, Takeda Castle, along the Sanindō toward Tottori, forms the most immediate threat. It is the stronghold of Ōtagaki Terunobu. Only a few years earlier, Terunobu had still been an ally of Nobunaga, but when, in 1573, the latter sent *Shōgun* Ashikaga Yoshiaki into exile, Terunobu had joined forces with the Mōri.

To deal with the threat from Terunobu and his Mōri allies, Hideyoshi sends his brother, Hidenaga, across the Mayumi Pass into Tajima Province at the head of a three-thousand-men-strong army to lay siege to Takeda Castle. For three days Terunobu manages to withstand the assault until, on the third night, he and the remainder of his men escape from the castle and flee westward to Yabu.

Hideyoshi himself, meanwhile, marches on Kōzuki Castle with the rest of his army. Though only a modest affair, the stronghold has good natural defenses. It sits on a mountain ridge along the west bank of the Sayo River, just a mile east of Harima's border with Bizen. From there, hidden paths

Old map of Kōzuki Castle on the west bank of the Sayo River

through the mountainous terrain provide ample opportunity for the Mōri to supply the castle with fresh weapons and provisions.

Hideyoshi's army arrives at Kōzuki Castle on 5 January 1578, some thirty-thousand of his men set up camp on the east bank of the Sayo River. Not willing to sacrifice them in a difficult assault, Hideyoshi sets up a cordon around the castle in three widening rings, thereby completely cutting off all the castle's supply lines into Bizen. The situation is hopeless for those within, and after just five days, the castle's lord, Akamatsu Masanori, commits ritual suicide along with his clan members and senior retainers. None of the castle's remaining defenders are spared by Hideyoshi's men. All those inside, including women and children, are put to the sword.

Having cleared the castle of its last defenders, Hideyoshi places the stronghold under the control of Amago Katsuhisa, a local chieftain whose clan has largely been wiped out by the Mōri.

It has taken Hideyoshi just two months to bring the provinces of Harima and Tajima under his control. At the end of January, during a formal occasion at Azuchi Castle, Nobunaga rewards his general with his treasured Otogoze-*gama*, a tea kettle only second to Matsunaga Hisahide's lost Hiragumo-*gama*.

MIKI & ITAMI

The sudden fall of Kōzuki Castle sends shockwaves through the ranks of the Mōri clan. It had proven their first serious foothold in Harima. Again Mōri Terumoto, who has now set up his headquarters at Matsuyama Castle in Bitchū, dispatches a force of some six thousand warriors toward Harima's border. At the same time, he manages to open up lines of communication with Bessho Nagaharu, the lord of Miki Castle in central Harima. Following Nobunaga's rise, the Bessho initially declared themselves on his side, and when Nobunaga launched his campaign to subdue the Ise Peninsula, Nagaharu dispatched one of his generals to take part. Nagaharu himself, however, remained behind at his stronghold of Miki Castle with the majority of his men. Terumoto knows that the chieftain's support for Nobunaga's campaign is only lukewarm at best. The Bessho, after all, have a long and proud history in the region, their chieftains having long occupied the rank of *shugo* or 'provincial governor' under the Kamakura *bakufu*. They at least expected to take the lead in Nobunaga's campaign and perhaps gain some territories along the way. Now they have been made to understand by Nobunaga (whom they consider only just their equal), that they are to submit to the will of his lieutenant Hideyoshi, a man of lowly birth and far below them.

The friction between the two parties comes to a head during a council toward the end of January at Kakogawa Castle between Hideyoshi and

Bessho Nagaharu (1558–80) ascended to the chieftaincy of his clan at the young age of twelve when, in 1570, his father Yasuhara fell in battle. Yasuhara was a man of great military talent who had managed to bring under his control much of eastern Harima Province. To do so, he had fought a constant battle with other powerful clans in the region, among them the Akamatsu and the Miyoshi. To strengthen his position, he had early on formed an alliance with Oda Nobunaga, who vied with the Miyoshi's for control of the capital Kyoto.

Five years after he had become his clan's chieftain, in the summer of 1575, Nagaharu, too, had an audience with Nobunaga to consolidate their alliance. Their alliance led to the Bessho clan participating in Nobunaga's campaign to pacify the Kii Peninsula.

The Bessho-Oda alliance, however, came under great pressure when Nobunaga launched his subsequent campaign to subdue the Chūgoku region, a region that included the province of Harima and the Bessho's hard-won territories. It was further undermined when he put his general Hashiba (Toyotomi) Hideyoshi in charge. Though a brilliant general, Hideyoshi was of humble origins and not attuned to the manners and customs of the western nobility. Gruff and uncivilized in his manners, he soon upset the already fraying relations between Nobunaga and his Harima allies. Expecting to play a profitable role in the operation, Nagaharu had initially gone along with Nobunaga's plans, but soon doubts began to creep in about his clan's position after the region's pacification.

Instrumental in the rift in the alliance was Nagaharu's uncle Yoshichika, who left no stone unturned to persuade his nephew to break with Nobunaga and instead form an alliance with the powerful Mōri. He was backed by most of Harima's indigenous clans, the so-called *kokujin*, whose origins went back to the local manors of the Kamakura period.

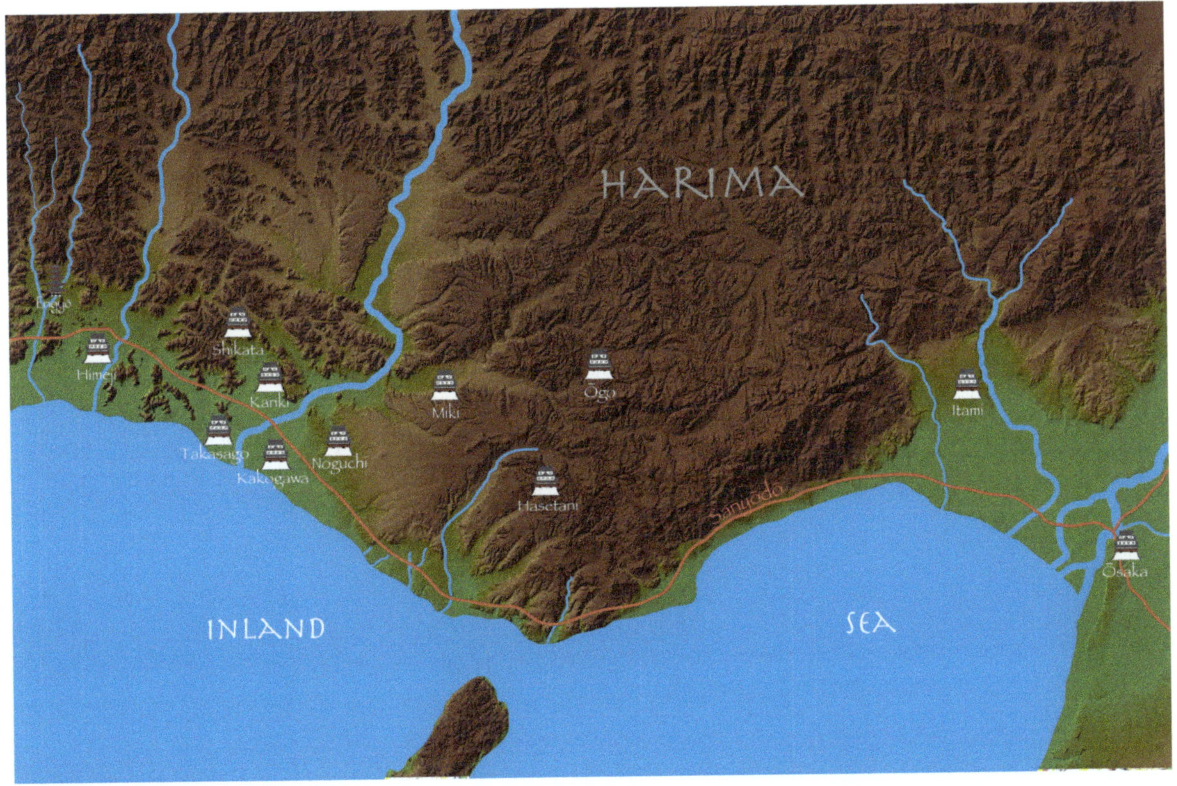

Nagaharu, who reproaches him for the indiscriminate slaughter over which he has presided at Kōzuki Castle. Hideyoshi is not the kind of man to feel any contrition for his actions, let alone apologize, and the two men part in a cloud of acrimony. It is at this point that Terumoto uses his line of communication with Nagaharu and persuades him to change sides. He succeeds. Shortly afterward, Nagaharu breaks off all communications with Hideyoshi and declares himself an ally to Mōri Terumoto.

By the time Hideyoshi returns from Azuchi Castle to deal with Nagaharu at Miki Castle, Mōri forces have already crossed the border and laid siege to Kōzuki Castle. Back at Azuchi Castle, Nobunaga becomes so concerned that he contemplates taking control of the Chūgoku campaign himself, but Sakuma Nobumori dissuades him from doing so. Instead, Nobunaga sends three of his generals—Akechi Mitsuhide, Takigawa Kazumasu, and Araki Murashige—toward Kōzuki Castle to relieve Amago Katsuhisa. On the night of 29 July 1578, they set up camp on the east bank of the Sayo River when they are ambushed by the Mōri and suffer a crushing defeat. Hideyoshi is inclined to come to their aid, but a missive from Nobunaga is clear and simple: their priority has switched from Kōzuki to Miki Castle. If Amago Katsuhisa and his men are to be sacrificed, so be it.

It is easy to abandon one castle; it is quite another thing to capture another. More than seven thousand battle-hardened warriors man the stockades of Miki Castle. And while the stronghold is not a *yamashiro*, a 'mountain castle,' like Kōzuki Castle, it is the next best thing: a *hirayamajō*, a stronghold partly built atop a hill, partly on the surrounding plane. The castle's inner citadel is situated atop a hill overlooking the Mino River, and is flanked on the north, south, and west by a number of walled baileys.

Contemporary map of Miki Castle

To complicate matters, Nagaharu's stronghold is surrounded by a ring of satellite castles whose lords have all chosen to join him in revolt. The first task for the besieging army, then, is to reduce these satellite castles. And there are many, as many as thirty in total. The most important guard Miki Castle's supply lines: Kanki and Shikata castles, ten miles west; Ōgo Castle, ten miles east; Takasago, Noguchi, and Ōzumi castles, roughly ten miles southwest along the coast of the Inland Sea; and Hasetani Castle, ten miles south. Thus begins a long and grinding battle to whittle away at this outer defensive ring.

The first satellite castle to fall is Noguchi Castle, which opens its gates on 12 May 1578. It is followed within days by Ōzu Castle, which stands in the way of Hideyoshi's main army. Then comes Kanki Castle, which surrenders on 19 August; then Shikata Castle, which surrenders on the first of September. Others manage to hold out. Among them are Takasago and Ōzumi castles, which are supported over water by Mōri ships and see in the New Year relatively unscathed. By then, the siege of Nagaharu's headquarters itself is already more than six months underway. To make matters worse, by the end of June, word reaches Hideyoshi's camp that, starved of help, Kōzuki Castle has fallen into the hands of the Mōri. Amago Katsuhisa and his remaining clansmen have committed *seppuku*.

The loss of Kōzuki Castle and Hideyoshi's failure so far to reduce Miki and a number of its satellite castles is the first major setback in Nobunaga's campaign to subdue western Honshu. It is followed in August by even more troubling news: Araki Murashige, one of the generals he has sent into Harima to relieve Kōzuki Castle, has also defected, and his reasons for doing so are similar to those of Bessho Nagaharu. Murashige, too, had initially followed Nobunaga's lead. He had fought hard alongside Akechi Mitsuhide's forces in the campaign against the Ishiyama Hongan-*ji*. But when Nobunaga had taken away his command and given it to Sakuma Nobumori he was left dismayed. That dismay turned into outright anger when he too was told to obey the orders of Hideyoshi—in his eyes a mere peasant. Following Nagaharu's example, Murashige returns to his family stronghold of Itami Castle (also known as Arioka Castle) and refuses to budge.

To Hideyoshi, who is encamped on the grounds of the Engyō Temple just north of Himeji, the effective loss of Itami Castle is even worse than the fall

The Engyō Temple

of Kōzuki Castle. Situated some thirty miles east of Miki Castle along the Sanyōdō, Itami Castle guards the gateway into Harima from the east. It also sits just north of the Ishiyama Hongan-*ji*, where the Ikkō sectarians are still holding out with the help of the Mōri over water. Indeed, Murashige, whose original seat had been nearby Hanakuma Castle, had captured the castle to put pressure on the sectarians in the first place. Now it has become yet another potential stronghold from which the Mōri can support the sectarians and put pressure on Nobunaga.

In an effort to bring Murashige back into the fold, Nobunaga dispatches Akechi Mitsuhide. Mitsuhide, after all, has married his daughter off to Murashige's oldest son, Muratsugu. If anyone can persuade Murashige that he cannot win this fight it is Mitsuhide. And it seems that Mitsuhide is successful. Murashige agrees to offer up his mother as a hostage to Nobunaga. The next day, he and his son set out from Itami Castle to escort her to Azuchi

Araki Murashige (1535–86) was the eldest son of Araki Yoshimura, the lord of Ikeda Castle in Settsu Province. Murashige began his military career as a vassal of the local Ikeda clan. But when, during the sixties, Settsu was invaded by the Miyoshi from Awa Province (in Shikoku), Murashige changed sides and captured the Ikeda territories for himself. His display of tactics during that campaign—especially his brilliant victory in the Battle of Shiraikawara (1571)—impressed Oda Nobunaga so much that he persuaded Murashige to join his side, even though the Ikeda were Nobunaga's allies and the Miyoshi his enemies.

Moving his headquarters to Ibaragi Castle in northern Settsu, Murashige's first years with Nobunaga were marked by a string of military successes, among them the capture of Kawae, Itami, Akutagawa, and Koshimizu castles. As a result, by the end of 1574, Murashige had gained control over all of Settsu Province.

Murashige also participated in Nobunaga's other campaigns. One of these was Nobunaga's almost obsessive campaign to root out the pernicious influence of the Ikkō sectarians, who had their power base in Echizen Province. In that campaign, Murashige contributed to most of the battles fought in Echizen, among others, the siege of Suizu, Itatori, and Hiri castles.

In Nobunaga's epic campaign against the Ikkō sectarian's vast fortifications at the Ishiyama Hongan-*ji*, too, Murashige played his part, specifically in the difficult siege of Takaya Castle, which required two lengthy battles that stretched over more than a year and saw the engagement of well over 100,000 men. He also took part in another major battle during the decade-long campaign, in the early summer of 1576, when some 15,000 Nobunaga troops attacked the sectarians' fortifications at Tennōji.

Murashige's next major contribution to Nobunaga's goal of Japan's pacification was his role in the campaign to subdue Kishū, to also root out the Ikkō sectarians there. This campaign, which affected the whole of the Kii Peninsula, was also directed against the menacing insurgencies of the warrior monks (*sōhei*) of the Negoro and Saika sects. It began in 1577, lasted until 1582, and saw the siege of a string of strongholds, culminating in an large-scale attack on the Shingon sect's bulwark atop Mt. Kōya. In reward for these contributions, Murashige was appointed governor of Settsu.

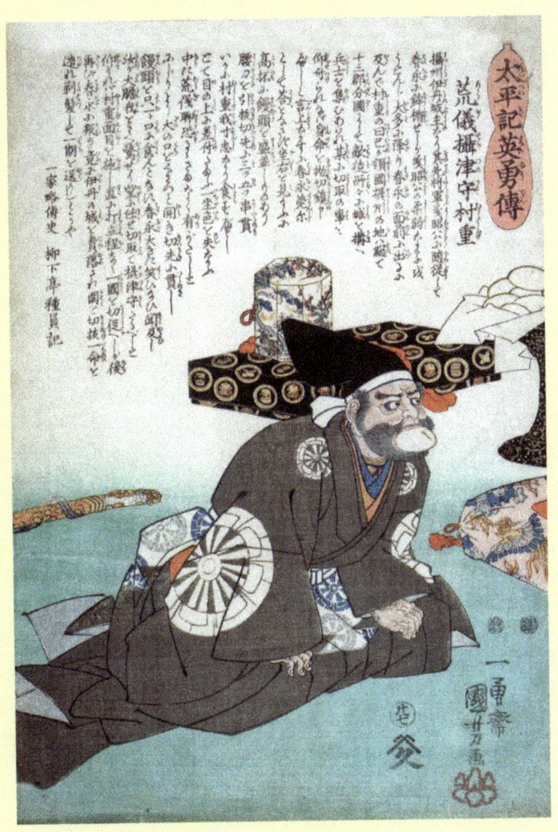

Contemporary map of Itami Castle

Castle. On their way there, they make a stopover at his son's castle of Ibaraki in Settsu. It is as far as they get. During a heated council that night, his senior retainers all express their disgust at their lordship's plan. It is madness, they argue, to let the old woman fall into Nobunaga's hands. The promised clemency is probably just a ruse; Nobunaga will have them all killed as soon as they enter Azuchi Castle. Instead, he should persist in his rebellion. If not, they will join the ranks of someone who will. And thus Murashige returns to his stronghold of Itami Castle. He does so reluctantly, for he knows the fate that awaits them. To try and bolster his position, Murashige instead sends hostages to Mōri Terumoto and Kōsa, the abbot of the Ishiyama Hongan-*ji*. Muratsugu's wife, on the other hand, is returned to her father, Mitsuhide.

In a last attempt to dissuade the rebel warlord from opposing Nobunaga, Kuroda Yoshitaka, who has long been close with Murashige, visits him at Itami Castle. But his plan backfires when Murashige takes his friend hostage.

Murashige's defection leaves Hideyoshi with some difficult choices. He cannot ignore Itami Castle as he did with Kōzuki Castle. To do so would expose his troops to an assault from the rear. On the other hand, at present, he only has some twenty thousand men at his disposal; to reduce Miki Castle he really needs twice the number. Now he is forced to split up his forces. And so, Oda Nobutada, who has thus far been assisting Hideyoshi in the siege, marches off toward Itami, leaving Hideyoshi with just over eight thousand men—only a few hundred more than those inside Miki Castle.

Oda Nobutada faces a similarly daunting task at Itami Castle as Hideyoshi at Miki Castle. Itami Castle is a formidable stronghold. Though built in the late 14th century, it has been under Murashige that the stronghold has been made into a base from which to combat the intransigent *sōhei* at the Ishiyama Hongan Temple. Measuring 1,500 by 700 yards it constitutes a narrow fortification along the west bank of the Ina River, at the place where travelers along the Sanyōdō have to ford the river. And, like Miki Castle, the stronghold is surrounded by a large number of satellite castles: Amagasaki and Ōwada, five miles south; Suita and Ibaraki, seven and ten miles east; Shinden, seven miles north; Maruyama and Sanda, fifteen miles west; and—most important of all—Hanakuma, seventeen miles east along the shore of the Inland Sea.

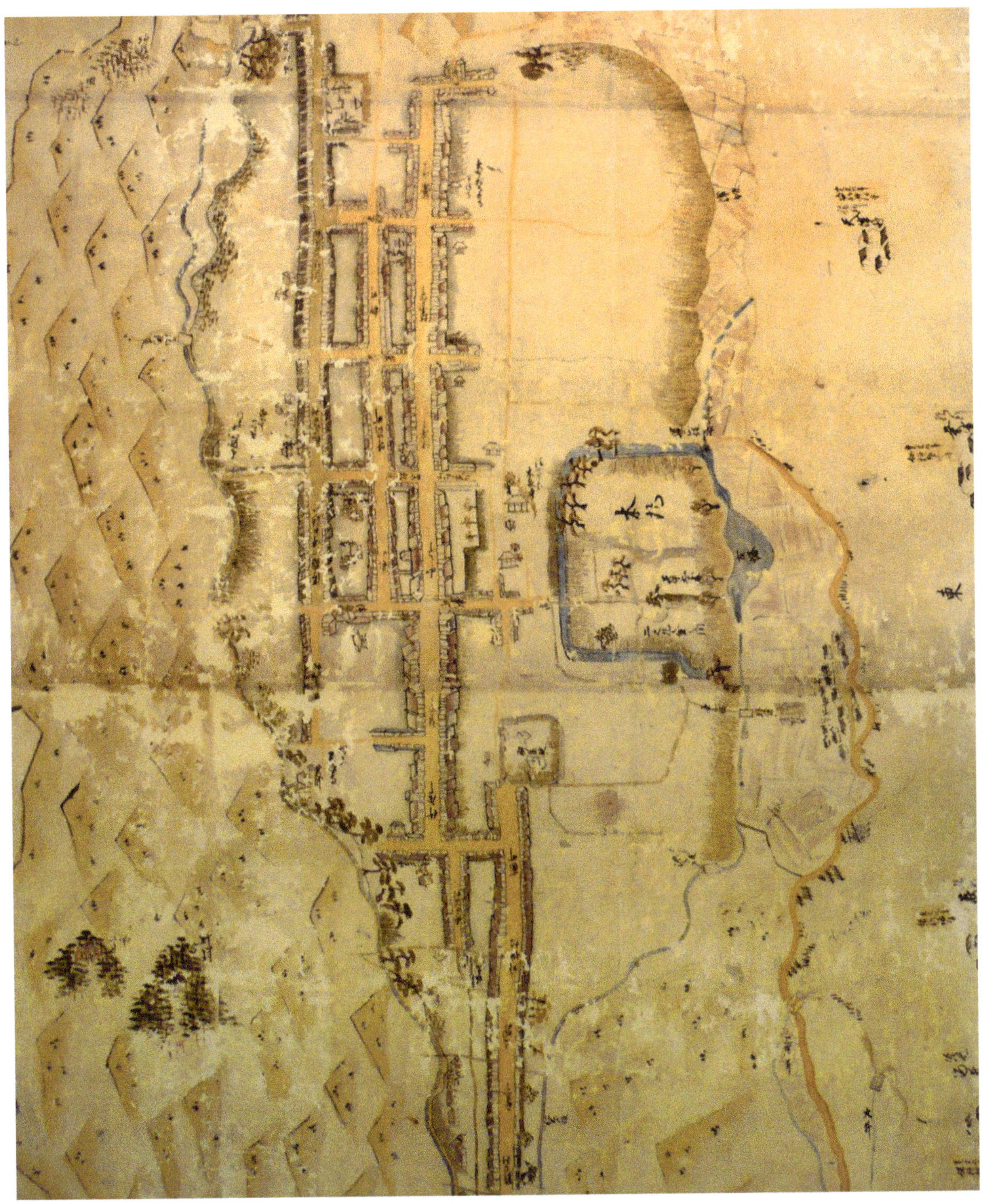

Far less skilled at siege warfare than Hideyoshi, Nobutada is not up to the task, and after some initial skirmishes, the stand-off settles into a protracted stalemate. The only true victory that fall, goes to Akechi Mitsuhide, who, on 27 November 1578, manages to capture Ibaraki Castle. Other successes are booked in less spectacular fashion when, one by one, Ōwada, Sanda, and Yamashita castles open their gates and surrender of their own volition.

Thus it is that Nobunaga's campaign to subdue the Chūgoku region enters its second year amid more setbacks than victories. To break the deadlock, Nobunaga decides to throw the majority of his forces into the campaign. Eventually, a vast army of some fifty thousand men descends on Itami Castle. On 12 December, they clash with one of Murashige's spearhead forces. The *Shinchō kōki* describes how:

> Our *ashigaru* having arrived, rushed forward under the command of Mutō Muneemon Kiyohide and clashed with the enemy forces. Muneemon cut through their ranks on horseback, returning in triumph with three enemy heads. And other allied commanders set fire to buildings in the vicinity of the castle, thus depriving its defenders of places to shelter during their sorties.

Shortly afterward, Nobunaga himself rides down from Azuchi and sets up his field headquarters at Ikeda, on the east bank of the Ina River, to conduct the siege of Itami Castle in person. His army attacks in full force on 5 January 1579, with an opening salvo of heavy-caliber cannon trained on the castle walls. It is followed by a hail of incendiary arrows, which set many of the castle town's thatched *buke yashiki* on fire. Yet those inside withstand the attack. In a series of sorties, they inflict huge casualties among the attacking forces, leaving as many as two thousand men dead in their wake, among them Manmi Shigemoto, one of Nobunaga's senior retainers.

After a week, there is still no sign the castle is about to fall. Nobunaga gets bored and departs again for Azuchi Castle to divert himself with falconry. Before he leaves, however, he orders his generals to change their strategy: Itami Castle is to be reduced by means of *hoshi-goroshi*, 'starvation

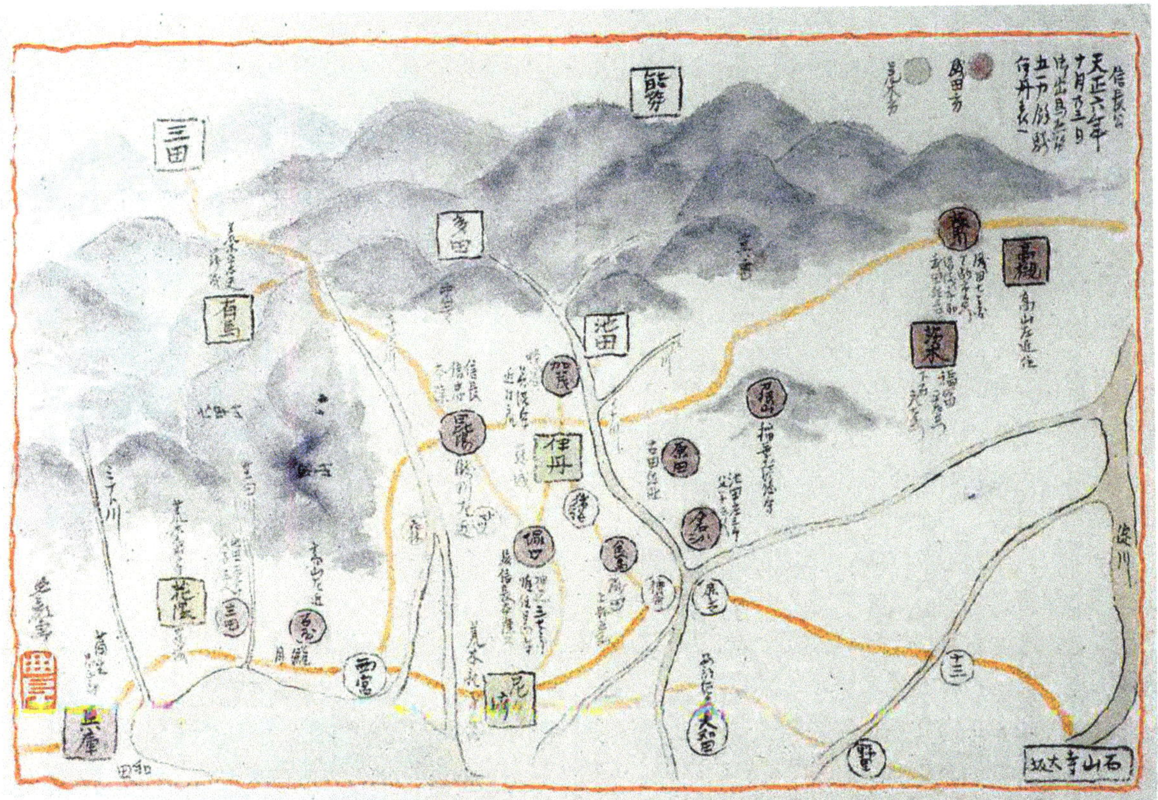

Itami Castle (center) and its satellites

through dehydration.' They duly comply, setting up a two-tier cordon around the castle.

For several weeks those inside the stronghold watch as they are being cut off from their supply lines. Then, on January 27, driven by hunger and a need to act, Murashige leads some five hundred of his strongest warriors in an attack against the Kamo-*toride*, a makeshift fort just north of Itami Castle, where Nobutada has set up his headquarters. The attack is so sudden that he and his men have to abandon the fort, causing their horses and provisions to fall into Murashige's hands.

It is the last effort Murashige undertakes to avert the inevitable. Finally, on 22 September of the same year, he and a small number of retainers escape from the castle under the cover of night. Boarding a small boat, they make their way down the Ina River toward Daimotsu Castle, one of the few satellite castles not yet captured by Nobunaga's forces. Itami Castle has been left under the control of its keeper, Ikeda Tomomasa. Nobutada offers him a way out, too: if he and his men are to surrender the castle, all the womenfolk and children will be spared. Tomomasa immediately departs in the direction of Daimotsu Castle—to try and persuade his master to surrender, he says. But instead, he flees to Awaji Island. Nobutada exacts his revenge with typical ruthlessness. The *Shinchō kōki* describes how, in the early morning of 30 December 1579:

> One hundred and twenty-two women and children were taken to Nanamatsu, just north of Daimotsu Castle, to be crucified. And like true wives of warriors of name, all the women were dressed in their finest since they knew the fate that awaited them. And from among these women, pliantly lined up in rows, the warriors violently grabbed one ofter the other, shoving their children into their arms, tied them to the crosses as they were, clutching their children in their arms. Then the warriors took their muskets and shot them one by one, and they proceeded to stab them to death with their *yari* and *naginata*. And the heavens echoed with the pitiful cries of these wailing women.

They are not the only ones who die that day. More than five hundred other women, as well as men, are put to death. They are not crucified but corralled into four houses that are then set ablaze. The only one inside the castle to survive the siege is Murashige's hostage, Kuroda Yoshitaka, who is safely returned to Himeji Castle. Araki Murashige himself ends his days in ignominy. Having forsaken his wife and children, he spends his remaining days as a Mōri tea master at Onomichi in western Honshu.

With Itami Castle again in his pocket, Nobunaga now turns the full brunt of his army against Miki Castle, which is still holding out after almost twenty months of encirclement. During that time, on 3 March 1579, Bessho Nagaharu and his younger brother, Harusada, have tried to break the siege by attacking Hideyoshi's camp atop Mt. Hirai, a mile due north of their stronghold. But now the parity in numbers works against them. They are unable to dislodge Hideyoshi's men and Harusada is killed in action. He is just eighteen years old. Five months later, on 30 September, the Mōri lead an attempt to resupply the castle by breaking through the cordon north of the castle. Led by Oishi Shōyū, they attack the forces of Tani Moriyoshi, who are dug in among makeshift fortifications atop Mt. Hirata, just north of the stronghold. At the same time, some three thousand Bessho men under the command of Nagaharu's uncle, Yoshichika, ford the Mino River and launch an attack on Moriyoshi's positions at nearby Ōmura. Heavy fighting ensues. By the end of the day, Moriyoshi is dead, as are a number of Bessho generals, but the blockade remains unbroken.

By January, the situation within the stronghold is dire. Nobunaga's tactics of *hoshi-goroshi* are taking effect: many have perished and many more are on the brink of starvation. Weakened by malnourishment, the castle's defenders are increasingly unable to man the barricades and put up a fight. One by one, the castle's baileys are reduced until, on the last day of January, only the inner citadel remains standing. By then, the Bessho clan leaders holed up inside have been given an ultimatum: if they are to commit *seppuku*, all their subjects will be spared. After a long council with his clan elders, Nagaharu concedes defeat. On 2 February 1580, he and his remaining brother, the twenty-year-old Tomoyuki, cut open their bellies in the castle's keep after

The siege of Miki Castle

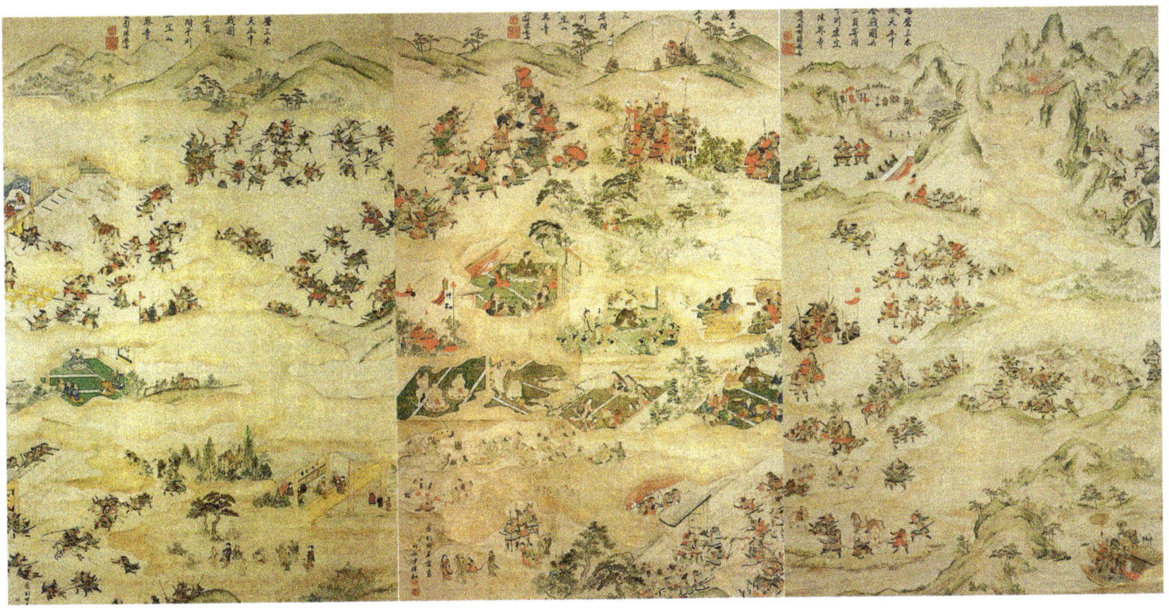

Nagaharu and his brother offer their lives to save those of their clansmen

they have put to death their womenfolk. His uncle Yoshichika, too, makes ready for his end. But at the last moment, he changes his mind and attempts to set fire to the keep. He is thwarted by Nagaharu's retainers, who put him to death and open the castle gates to Hideyoshi's forces. The official records claim that this time around, Hideyoshi keeps his word. But letters from his commanders in the field paint a different picture; they state that all those remaining in the castle are put to the sword.

TOTTORI

With Harima firmly under Nobunaga's control, the stage is now set for what will become the next major siege in his campaign to subdue western Honshu: the siege of Tottori Castle. Among all the strongholds in the Chūgoku region, Tottori Castle in Inaba Province (Tottori Prefecture) boasts the most formidable natural defenses. Like Matsunaga Hisahide's Shigisan Castle, it is a traditional *yamashiro*, sitting atop Kyūshō-*yama*, a 263 m high hill, just where the Sanindō makes a sharp turn inland from the coast to cross the Sendai River. Though the stronghold itself consists of little more than a small inner citadel flanked by a second bailey on the east, it is surrounded by thick stockades and can only be approached along a steep road that winds its way up the hill's southern slope and is guarded by *toride* or small 'forts' at several stages along the way.

The lord of Tottori Castle is Yamana Toyokuni. Though in name the governor of Inaba, Toyokuni has had great trouble in keeping the province under his control. In truth, it has been a painful balancing act, a constant struggle to negotiate the volatile forces at play in the region. He has tried to appease Mōri Terumoto, even taking on part of his name (moto) and renaming himself Yamana Mototoyo. It hasn't worked. Seven years earlier, the Mōri invaded Inaba and captured his castle. It is only recently that he has been able to regain control of Tottori Castle. This time around, he has

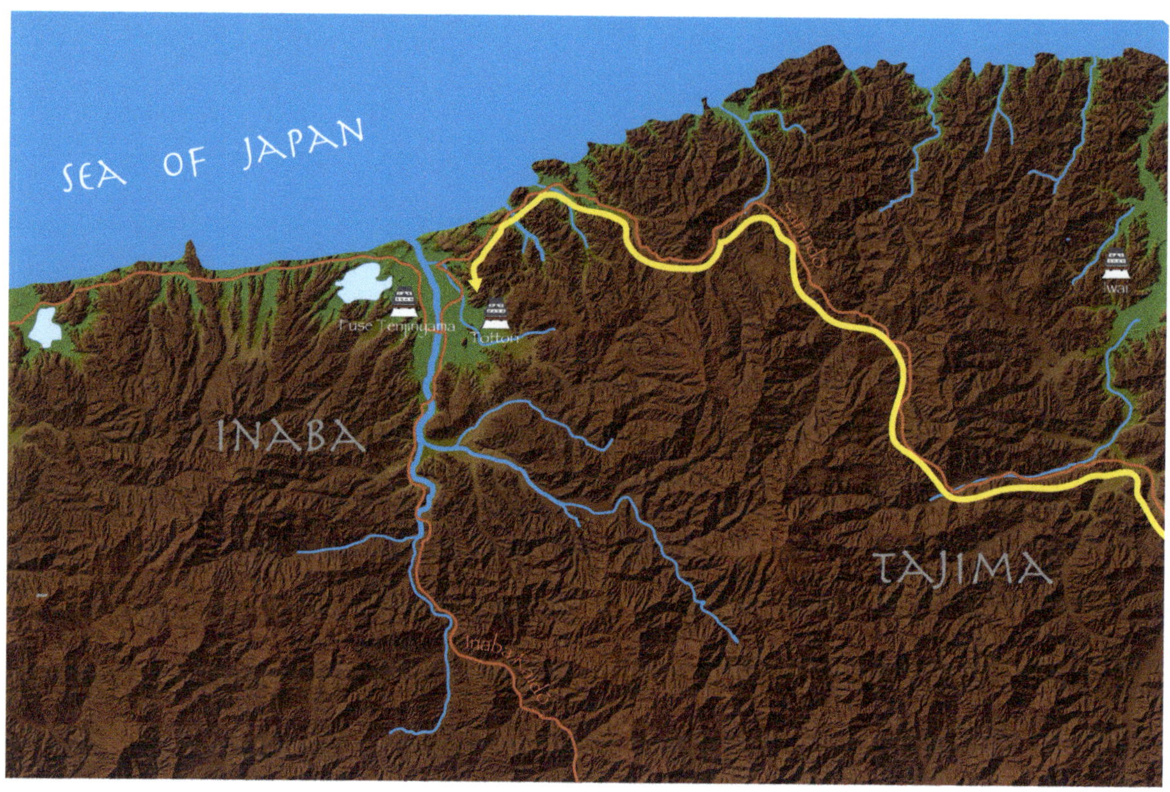

sought to establish friendly relations with Oda Nobunaga, abandoning his new name as a sign of his commitment. But this, too, goes up in smoke when, in early August 1580, Hideyoshi marches into Inaba and lays siege to Tottori Castle. At first, Toyokuni is inclined to open his castle's gates on the condition that he can retain control of Inaba. But two of his elders, Morishita Dōyo and Nakamura Harutsugu, vehemently argue against it. They know Nobunaga's reputation and fear his promises are worth little more than the paper they are written on. 'Look at the fate of those at Itami and Miki castles,' they argue, 'what has become of them?' Toyokuni is dissuaded and the castle doors remain closed.

For three months, egged on by his belligerent elders, Toyokuni resists Hideyoshi's repeated attempts at a negotiated settlement. But toward the end of October, he overrules their protestations and surrenders his castle on the condition he can remain in control of Inaba Province.

Yamana Toyokuni (1548–1626) was the second son of Yamana Toyosada, a chieftain from Tajima. During the first half of the 16th century, Toyosada had invaded neighboring Inaba Province and brought much of its eastern part under his control. To govern his newly won territories, he had made Fuse Tenjinyama Castle his new headquarters.

When Toyosada passed away in 1560, the chieftaincy of the Yamana clan went to Toyokuni's elder brother Toyokazu, who installed himself at his father's headquarters of Tenjinyama Castle as governor of Inaba Province. Toyokuni was initially granted the satellite stronghold of Iwai Castle, which stood some fifty miles east of Tottori Castle and controlled the eastern part of Tajima. Before long, however, the two brothers fell out. Toyokazu and his senior councilor, Takeda Takanobu, evicted Toyokuni from his stronghold and forced him to flee across the border. Just a few years later, in 1564, Takanobu, who had his headquarters at nearby Tottori Castle, rose against his master and slew Toyokazu.

For almost a decade Toyokuni had to bide his time while Takanobu maintained a tentative sway over Inaba from Tottori Castle. But when, in 1573, Toyokuni manages to forge an alliance with the local Yamana and Amago clans, he and his allies finally managed to evict Takanobu from his stronghold after a siege that lasted almost two months.

No sooner had Toyokuni installed himself at Tottori Castle as Inaba's new governor, than his stronghold was attacked by the Mōri commander Kikkawa Motoharu. Unlike the stronghold's former lord, Toyokuni hardly put up a fight, and after a short siege, he submitted to Mōri rule. In reward for his subjugation, he was allowed to hang on to his castle and granted his new name of Mototoyo, which borrowed the last character (moto) from the name of the powerful Mōri chieftain Mōri Terumoto.

With matters settled, Hideyoshi returns to his headquarters of Himeji Castle in Harima. But no sooner have his forces left Inaba than Toyokuni's two senior elders evict their lord from the castle and declare themselves for the Mōri. They now call on the help of Kikkawa Motoharu, one of Nobunaga's fiercest opponents in the region. The lord of Hinoyama Castle in Aki Province (Hiroshima Prefecture), Motoharu had been part of the Mōri alliance that had recaptured Kōzuki Castle. He replies to the elders' call for

Contemporary map of Tottori Castle and its castle town

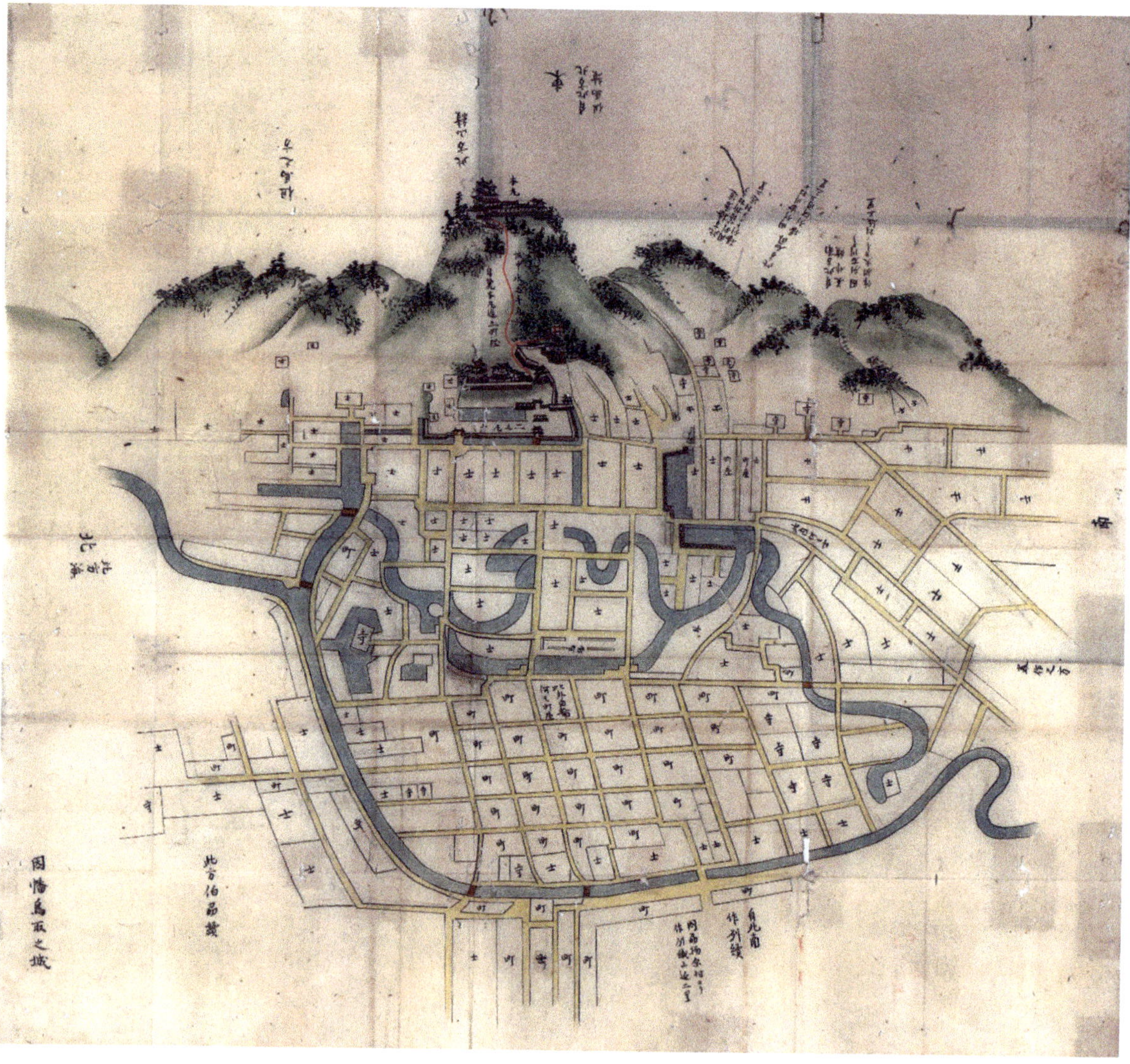

help by sending his cousin Kikkawa Tsuneie, the lord of Fukumitsu Castle in Iwami, some one hundred and fifty miles east of Tottori. Tsuneie arrives at Tottori Castle in early April of the next year, 1581, and together the three men raise the banner of revolt.

Hideyoshi is far from pleased with the ease with which Toyokuni has let himself be robbed of his castle a second time. He is also frustrated with his own performance. This is the second time, too, that he has let a captured castle fall back into the hands of the Mōri. At this pace, the subjugation of western Honshu will take an eternity. And so he once again marches into Inaba to lay siege to Tottori Castle, this time at the head of an army of some twenty thousand men.

Arriving on the north coast of Honshu near Tottori on the night of 27 June, Hideyoshi convenes a war council with his commanders. He instructs them to set up a cordon around the castle. Before doing so, however, they are to drive all those who live in the vicinity up toward the stronghold, forcing them to join its defenders. It is a measure that is bound to put all the more pressure on the limited food supplies within the castle once it has been cut off. To make sure that those inside the stronghold will not be able to replenish their supplies, his commanders are to impound all merchant ships that call at the mouth of the river, only letting them go once their merchants have bought up all of the remaining rice supplies at double the going rate.

The next morning, Hideyoshi climbs a high mountain some five miles due east from the castle and makes his men set up his field headquarters on its western slope facing the castle.

Recording the events of that summer in Hideyoshi's first official biography, the *Taikō-ki*, the retainer (of Hideyoshi's nephew, Hidetsugu) and Confucianist scholar Oze Hoan describes how:

> When the bell at Hideyoshi's main camp sounded, the large *taiko* drums at each commander's encampment, as well as the many small *taiko* drums atop the turrets replied as one, causing a tremendous clamor. And at night the whole area was illuminated with lanterns and torches, causing all hope within the castle that they might soon receive help from the outside to be extinguished.

Hideyoshi purveys the siege of Tottori Castle

They have good reason to lose hope. Hideyoshi's cordon around the castle is hermetic. By the time his men are finished, an eight-foot-deep trench stretches west of the castle for almost ten miles. Behind it, they have erected an equally high wooden palisade that is interspersed with three-story watch-towers at five-mile intervals and completely encircles the castle. Each section in between is manned by twenty mounted warriors, one hundred sharp-shooters, and a hundred more regular *teppō ashigaru*. At every three miles stands a guardhouse manned with shifts of fifty to sixty guards who patrol the perimeter night and day. As a result, the whole area around the castle is 'teeming with men like ants like the vast numbers of pilgrims that used to visit the Kumano shrine in the old days, leaving not a crevice open.'

On the water, too, Hideyoshi exerts his control. Using boats as pontoons, he builds a bridge across the Sendai River, both to send his men across and

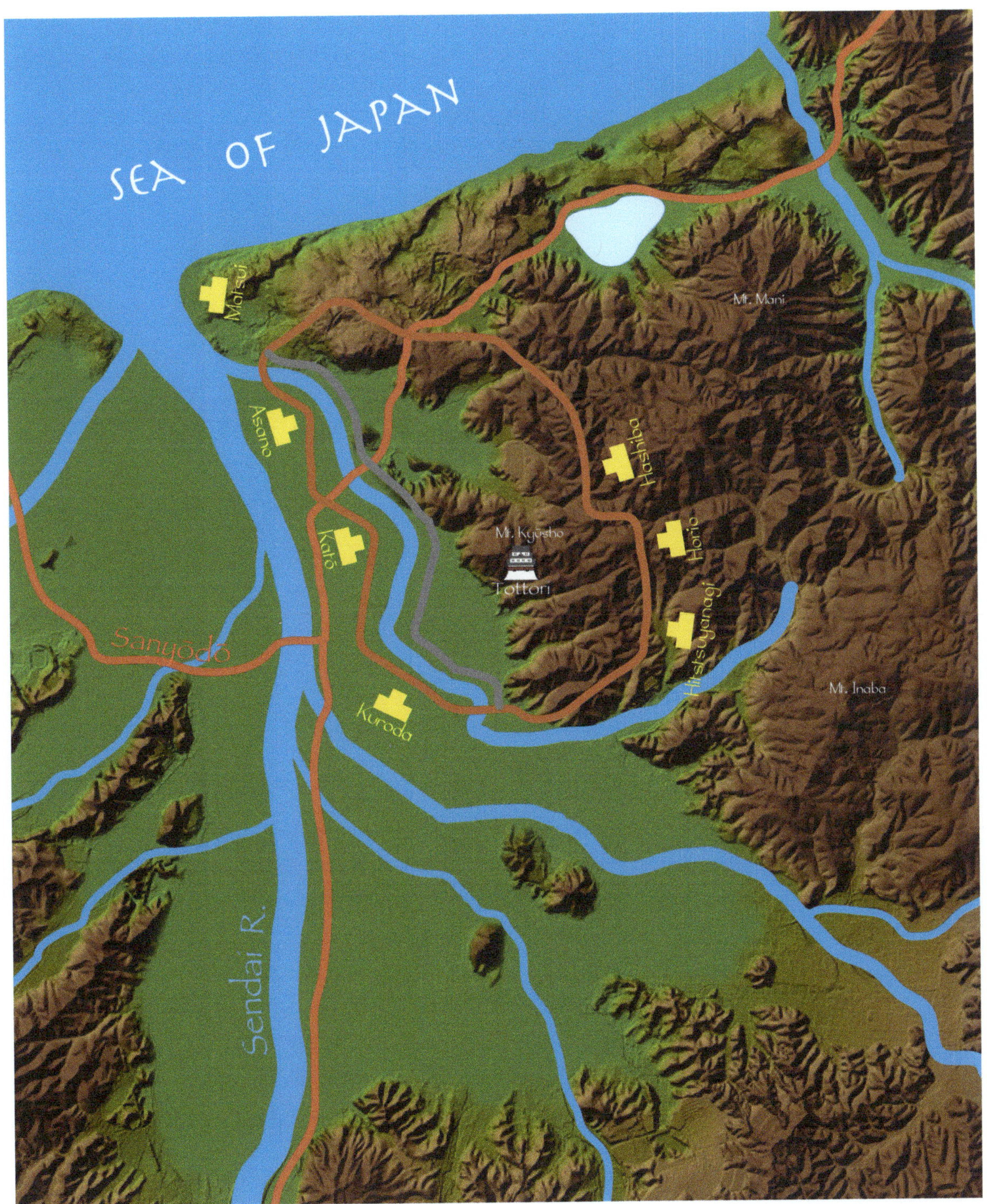
SEA OF JAPAN
Matsui
Mt. Mani
Asano
Hashiba
Mt. Kyūsho
Tottori
Katō
Horio
Hitstsuyanagi
Sanyōdō
Kuroda
Mt. Inaba
Sendai R.

The harrowing scenes within the walls of Tottori Castle

to block all traffic up the river. Out at sea, meanwhile, a fleet of warships under the command of Matsui Yasuyuki, patrols the Inaba coastline on the constant lookout for any Mōri ships sent to Tsuneie's aid. These are spotted on 13 October that year. That same day, both forces clash at the mouth of the Sendai River. The sea battle ends in the defeat of the Mōri forces and the death of their commander Kanoashi Mototada.

By that time, Hideyoshi's multi-pronged strategy is already putting enormous strains on the castle's food supplies, which can no longer be supplemented with locally grown or imported cereals. They are merely calculated to support its fourteen-hundred-strong garrison, not a large number of additional peasant families. As a result, their ranks have been swelled to an unsustainable four thousand, the majority not even fighting men. Within weeks, and despite only meager rations, all the livestock, horses, and foodstuffs have been exhausted. At first, footmen had been sent out at five-day intervals to go and cut down the foliage around the castle. Upon their return, the womenfolk would then sift through the paltry harvest in the hope of finding a few remaining rice stalks. By now, the slopes around the castle are barren and all within are on the brink of starvation. The *Shinchō kōki* describes how:

> Both men and women, so utterly thin and worn out by hunger that they looked like little children, drew near the stronghold's stockades, calling out in their agony to those without, pleading with them and begging them to withdraw and thereby save their souls; and their cries were filled with such agony that it was impossible to look on without being moved by pity.

Some within the stronghold are even driven to eat from the remains of the dead. The most gruesome scenes, however, take place outside the castle walls, along the palisades erected by Hideyoshi's men. The *Taikō-ki* describes how:

> The emaciated wretches who sought to escape the castle by climbing the palisades were being picked off by our *teppō ashigaru*. Upon this, hungry women and men alike crowded in upon them en masse and began to dismember them with their swords, sickles, and lances, even while they were still alive and breathing—it was as if a butcher were shedding a cow or horse from its hide.

After another month, the relentless suffering in and around Tottori Castle becomes too much to bear for the castle's keeper, Kikkawa Tsuneie, and the two elders. On 19 November, Fukumitsu Kosaburō, one of Tsuneie's most trusted men, is sent to Hideyoshi's camp with a proposal: all three leaders are ready to offer their lives in return for the lives of those in their care and under their command.

Kosaburō reaches the encampment of Asano Nagamasa, one of Hideyoshi's Five Commissioners. The latter brings him to Hideyoshi's camp east of Tottori Castle, where he is allowed to make his case before the *Taikō-sama*. Never a man to waste the lives of his men without good cause,

Hideyoshi agrees and instructs Nagamasa to reply favorably in writing. That same evening, Kosaburō returns to the castle with Nagamasa's letter:

> To Master Fukumitsu Kosaburō,
>
> I have presented your case to Lord Hideyoshi. And his lordship was moved by the proposal that all three masters of the castle lay down their lives in exchange for the lives of all the others. He will forthwith send ten carts of food with five sorts of fish by way of relief. Please inform your lords he is firmly committed to upholding his promise.
>
> Asano Yahei Nagamasa

Two days later, on 21 November 1581, Kikkawa Tsuneie, Morishita Dōyo, and Nakamura Harutsugu take their lives by ritual suicide, having prepared the very buckets in which their heads will be collected. The three heads are delivered to Hideyoshi. Even he is moved by their valiant resistance and weeps at the sight of the emaciated heads, exclaiming, '*Awarenaru gishi kana!*' (How sad the plight of the loyal retainer!). He has Tsuneie's head pickled and sent to Nobunaga, who is then at Azuchi Castle and who arranges for Tsuneie's remains to have a dignified burial.

This time, Hideyoshi, makes good on his promise. All those inside the castle, including the wives and children of the three leaders, are spared. And in a rare display of compassion, he instructs his men to nurse all the survivors back to health. Knowing that too much food after such a long time of starvation will kill them, he instructs his men to prepare large cauldrons of rice gruel which is to be fed to the survivors in small portions at a time. And to the villages around the castle, he sends some three hundred *koku* of rice to get through the winter.

BITCHŪ TAKAMATSU

The next stage in Hideyoshi's conquest of the Chūgoku region is the pacification of its central provinces of Mimasaka, Bizen, and Bitchū (all of them present-day Okayama Prefecture). Setting out from Himeji Castle on 7 April 1582 with a force of twenty thousand men, he crosses the border of Bizen. Bizen, at this time, is still largely Ukita territory. Only a month earlier, their leader, Ukita Naoie, who had been allied to the Mōri, has passed away at his headquarters of Okayama Castle on the west bank of the Asahi River. His successor, Hideie, is only ten years old. Leadership of the clan has temporarily been assumed by his uncle Tadaie, the master of Kameyama Castle, which stands east of Okayama Castle, just ten miles from the border. Tadaie commands some ten thousand men, and it is on his initiative that the Ukita abandon their alliance with the Mōri. In return for continued control of their territories, Tadaie agrees to join Hideyoshi's army. On 7 May, a force of some thirty thousand men crosses the border with Bitchū and descends on Takamatsu Castle, one of the Mōri's most formidable strongholds in central Chūgoku.

Takamatsu Castle is the stronghold of Shimizu Muneharu, a staunch ally of the Mōri. He controls some five thousand men defending a stronghold that poses a serious challenge to Hideyoshi's genius in siege warfare. Situated in the delta of the Takahashi River, on the east bank of one of its tributaries,

the Ashimori River, the flat plain castle is in effect a water fortress. The *Taikō-ki* describes it as such:

> Takamatsu Castle is surrounded on three sides by deep marshes that stretch on for miles and miles, impenetrable for both horses and men. It is all the more so for men advancing clad in heavy suits of armor and helmets. On its one exposed side, the castle is protected by deep water-filled trenches that emanate from the castle in multiple rings. The Mōri have spent many years in hard labor to build this castle and it is not a stronghold that can be reduced in the course of a few months, even by brute force.

Consulting with his adviser Kuroda Yoshitaka, Hideyoshi, who has set up camp at the foot of Mt. Ryūō, immediately north of the castle, decides on a different course of action: a *mizu-zeme* or 'water attack.' They are to take the castle's strength and turn it against it. That strength is water. If they are to stem the flow of the Ashimori River and cause the low-lying area to flood, the castle will be inundated. Moreover, soon the rainy season will be upon them; if they hurry, the effect of their strategy will be all the more dramatic.

In charge of the project is Hachisuka Masakatsu, a longstanding Nobunaga retainer whose clan controls all transport on the Kiso River, which runs below Nobunaga's stronghold of Gifu Castle. At Yoshitaka's direction, Masakatsu sets to work erecting a dam that cuts across the Ashimori River from high land at Kawazugahana, just south of the castle. From there, it is to closely follow the west bank of the river, all the way north toward Monzen, roughly a mile north of the castle. Masakatsu mobilizes a vast workforce, many of them soldiers, but also a large number of locally recruited peasants, who are paid the princely sum of one hundred *sen* for each bag of sand they contribute. Work begins at the end of May. When it is completed just twelve days later, the dam stretches for more than three miles at an average height of fifteen feet and a width of thirty.

The siege of Takamatsu Castle

Shimizu Muneharu (1537–82) was the second son of Shimizu Munenori, the lord of Shimizu Castle. The Shimizu, at the time of Muneharu's birth, was only a small clan with little influence. Munenori, whose stronghold stood on the east bank of the Asahi River in southern Bichū Province, was a vassal of the Mimura, a clan that hailed from far away Hitachi Province but had settled in Bitchū during the 12th century.

The Mimura (whose headquarters of Matsuyama Castle stood in central Bitchū) were, in turn, closely related through intermarriage to the Ishikawa, from whose ranks the hereditary governor of Bitchū was drawn. The governor at the time Muneharu came of age was Ishikawa Hisataka, and it was not long afterward that Muneharu married one of Hisataka's daughters and switched his allegiance from the Mimura to the Ishikawa.

As the governor of Bitchū, Ishikawa Hisataka established his headquarters at Takamatsu Castle, a stronghold he built during the middle of the 16th century. Muneharu, who was now his son-in-law and confidant, was given control of Kōzan Castle, a small satellite stronghold that stood just a few miles west of Takamatsu Castle.

When, in 1575, Hisataka passed away after a short illness, the keys to Takamatsu Castle went to his son Ishikawa Hisanori. But, in that same year, disaster struck when the Mōri invaded Bitchū Province. Hisanori and his cousin Mimura Motochika frantically sought to halt the Mōri advance, as one by one their strongholds in western Bitchū were overrun. Eventually, they ensconced themselves in Matsuyama Castle but on 7 July 1575, after a siege that had lasted for more than a month, their stronghold fell, and Hisanori and Motochika committed ritual suicide.

Muneharu, who at this time was still in control of nearby Kōan Castle, entered into negotiations with Kobayakawa Takakage, the Mōri commander who had led the siege of Matsuyama Castle. Takakage responded positively to Muneharu's overtures, and over the next few years Muneharu participated in the Mōri campaign to expand their influence eastward. It was during this campaign that Muneharu increasingly won Takakage's trust and that, in reward for his service, he was awarded the control of Takamatsu Castle.

Hideyoshi observes the siege from a tower at the foot of Mt. Ryūō

When the rain finally comes, the river soon turns into a mighty stream. Blocked downstream at Kawazugahana and hemmed in from the west, it bursts its eastern bank, causing the low-lying flatlands and marshes around the castle to be flooded. The rising water seeps into the castle's outer baileys, forcing those within to move from place to place by means of small boats. With each day the water levels continue to rise and before long, even the inner citadel and its buildings are flooded. Carpenters are put to work to raise the floors, but to little avail, according to the *Taikō-ki*:

> The most terrifying was the vermin—the snakes, rats, and weasels—that now freely began to creep above the floorboards in great numbers, causing women and children to faint in terror. At first, they would call out crying for help until at length, having grown accustomed to the sight, even they remained quiet.

Yet despite the increasingly desperate situation, those within the castle stubbornly hold out. In a bid to save his men, Shimizu Muneharu dispatches the monk and diplomat Ankokuji Ekei toward Hideyoshi's camp by boat to

Ekei pleads with Hideyoshi

try and reach a negotiated settlement. He instructs the monk that he is willing to cede control over the provinces of Bitchū, Bingo, Mimasaka, Hōki, and Izumo in return for their lives. Hideyoshi turns the offer down. He wants Muneharu's head.

Even while those within the castle are mulling over Hideyoshi's counteroffer, their hopes are raised when, during the first days of June, word reaches the castle that a relief force sent by Mōri Terumoto has arrived. It is a double vanguard force under the command of Kikkawa Motoharu, and Kobayamawa Takakage, who set up their camps atop Mt. Hizashi and Mt. Iwazaki respectively. A week later, Terumoto arrives at the head of the main force and sets up his headquarters at the old stronghold of Sarukake, some ten miles west along the Sanyōdō.

Hideyoshi, who has meanwhile moved his headquarters to Mt. Ishii, just east of the castle, in an effort to counter this new threat, grows increasingly restless. His scouts tell him that the combined Mōri forces outnumber him by two to one, perhaps even more. If he is to keep the pressure on, he needs at least the same number of men. On 5 June, he sits down to write a letter to Nobunaga to explain the situation:

> My lord, please allow me to briefly explain in writing the situation on the ground here at Takamatsu Castle.
>
> I have secured the terrain. With many brave and capable commanders at my disposal, I have subjected the castle to a *mizu-zeme* and I expect the stronghold to fall within a few dozen days.
>
> However, Mōri Terumoto has now arrived at the head of a relief force running in the tens of thousands of mounted warriors. He has taken up positions opposite our troops at a distance of no more than five miles and is set on saving Takamatsu Castle.
>
> If your lordship were to send at least some reinforcements to help in the siege of Takamatsu Castle, we will be able to thoroughly route the Mōri in battle—if it were to come to that—and thereby bring the west of the country under our control within the year.
>
> Hashiba Chikuzen no Kami Hideyoshi

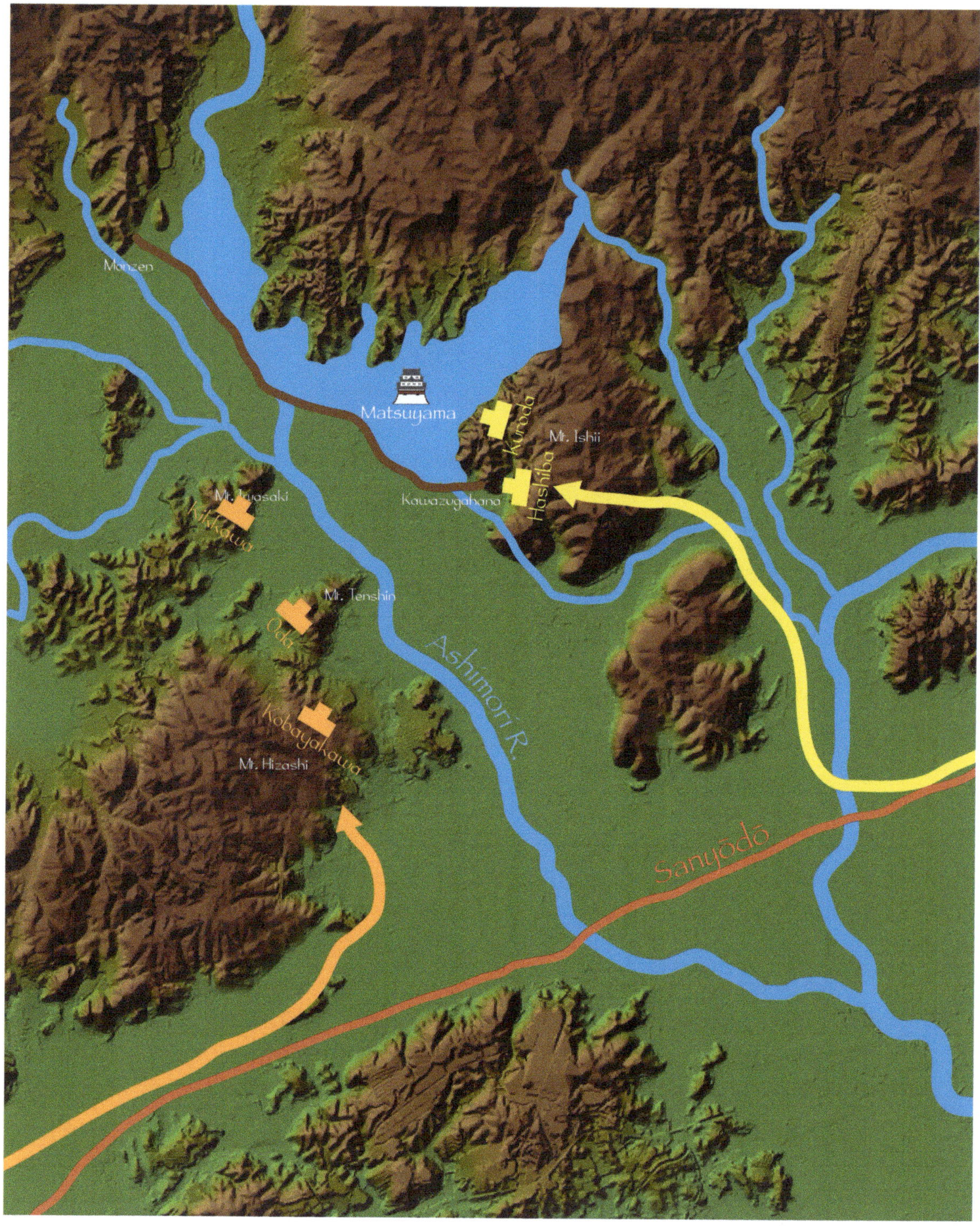
Monzen
Matsuyama
Kuroda
Mt. Ishii
Hashiba
Kawazugahana
Mt. Iwasaki
Kikkawa
Mt. Tenshin
Oda
Ashimori R.
Kobayakawa
Mt. Hizashi
Sanyōdō

Hideyoshi's letter has the desired effect. Nobunaga, who is in the middle of entertaining his ally Tokugawa Ieyasu at Azuchi Castle when the letter arrives, immediately swings into action. That same day, he sends word to Hideyoshi that he has ordered Akechi Mitsuhide to prepare a large force to come to Hideyoshi's aid.

For two weeks Hideyoshi impatiently waits for Nobunaga's reinforcements to arrive. Then, late in the evening of June 22, well after dark, his men intercept a messenger trying to make his way to the enemy camp. It is a stroke of incredibly good luck. The man turns out to be Fujita Denpachirō, a retainer of Akechi Mitsuhide, and on him, he carries a letter to Mōri Terumoto. The content of the letter lands like a bombshell: In it, Mitsuhide reveals that he is plotting to move against his lord Nobunaga at his residence on the grounds of the Honnō Temple in Kyoto. Moreover, he encourages Mōri Terumoto to hold out until he has succeeded in his mission. As soon as he has killed Nobunaga, he will come to their aid so that they can deal with Hideyoshi together.

Hideyoshi is stunned, not in the least by Mitsuhide's unbelievable treachery. It also puts his forces in a very dangerous position. Already he has trouble holding off the Mōri. Now, instead of the much-needed reinforcements, he is threatened from the rear. If Mitsuhide succeeds and launches an attack against him from the east, he will be pincered between two powerful forces.

The news has turned Hideyoshi's plans totally upside down. His chief priority at this point is to return to his headquarters of Himeji Castle. There he will have to see whether Mitsuhide has indeed risen in revolt and whether he has succeeded in his mission to topple Nobunaga. If so, his advisor Yoshitaka argues, Hideyoshi should do all he can to punish the wayward Mitsuhide. An alliance between him and the Mōri is not only bound to thwart their mission to pacify western Japan; it might well pose a serious challenge to their control of central Japan and undo all Nobunaga's hard-earned accomplishments.

Of course, it is of paramount importance that the news be kept from the Mōri as long as possible. As long as they are in the dark about Mitsuhide's revolt, Hideyoshi will still have a decent hand in his negotiations with those within the castle. So as to keep the news from spreading outside the circle

Muneharu takes receipt of Hideyoshi's gifts

of his close advisers, Hideyoshi immediately enacts a gagging order on his men: anyone who will leak the news will pay for it with his life. With some luck, it will create a small window of opportunity to reach a settlement with the Mōri—a settlement without which he will not be able to withdraw his forces to Himeji to deal with Mitsuhide.

Early next morning, June 23, his commissioner Asano Nagamasa ferries over toward the castle with Hideyoshi's new counteroffer: they only have to cede the provinces of Bitchū, Mimasaka, and Hōki. Shimizu Muneharu, however, still has to offer his life. In return, Hideyoshi will spare all those who serve under him. To Hideyoshi's great relief, his offer is accepted. As he did at Tottori Castle, he sends Horio Yoshiharu over to the castle with a present of *sake* and fish to serve as Muneharu's last meal.

Later that morning, at the hour of the Snake, having enjoyed his last meal, Muneharu ferries over to Hideyoshi's camp. There he performs a *nō* dance and recites his death poem:

Leaving this fleeting world behind
The name and fame of a warrior
Are no more than the mosses
On the walls of Takamatsu Castle.

Then, sitting down opposite Hideyoshi, he commits ritual suicide by disemboweling himself. He is not the only one to die: his brother, Munetomo, too, dies by his own sword, as do two of their most trusted retainers.

The next day, June 24, Hideyoshi and Kuroda Yoshitaka sit down with the monk Ankokuji Ekei to work out the details of the peace settlement with the Mōri. To his great relief, they are not yet aware of Mitsuhide's revolt. During their negotiations, it is decided that the extent of the Mōri territories will be reduced to the area east of the Takahashi River and west of the Yawata River. Hostages, too, are to be exchanged: two from Mōri Terumoto's side; two from Hideyoshi's side. When all is put in writing and sealed in blood, Hideyoshi orders Hachisuka Masakatsu to breach the dam at Kawazugahana. Then orders are sent out to all his commanders in the field to lift the siege and depart for Himeji before the next day is out.

Setting out from Takamatsu Castle the next afternoon, June 25, his army travels east along the Sanyōdō throughout the night without rest and at such

Muneharu makes ready to meet his end

a breakneck speed that they reach Himeji before dusk has set in the next evening—they have covered the fifty miles stretch in less than a day. By now the rainy season has begun and though the weather is atrocious, their task has been lightened by Hideyoshi's decision to transport provisions and arms over the Inland Sea toward the port of Akashi. Known as the Chūgoku Daigaeshi, or the Great Return from Chūgoku, this remarkable feat is the most impressive forced march in Japanese military history.

By the time Hideyoshi himself reaches Himeji Castle, he already knows that his worst fears have come true. Five days earlier, on the morning of 21 June, Mitsuhide has attacked Nobunaga at the Honnō Temple. Nobunaga is dead, killed at his own hand after a short and desperate standoff.

Ten days later, Mitsuhide, too, is dead, his forces routed by Hideyoshi in the Battle of Yamasaki. It leaves Hideyoshi in de facto control of the country—at least the central and western part that has been pacified. It is now left to him to complete Nobunaga's mission of unifying the whole country.

ODAWARA

By the year 1590 Hideyoshi has made great strides toward fulfilling Nobunaga's goal. He has pacified the whole of the Chūgoku region by signing a pact with the Mōri and subjugated the islands of Shikoku and Kyūshū. Yet the eastern Kantō and the northeastern Tōhoku regions are still very much the domain of mutually contending warlords. One of them is Date Masamune, who seeks to control of northeastern Japan. In the Kantō it is the Hōjō who dominate the scene. Their founder is Ise Shinkurō, a ruthless local warrior who gained control of the Izu Peninsula toward the end of the fifteenth century. Bent on overthrowing the Muromachi *bakufu*, he took on the name of Hōjō Sōun, after the illustrious Hōjō who had eclipsed the Minamoto, thus founding the so-called Later Hōjō.

With the demise of Takeda Shingen and Uesugi Kenshin, all serious challengers to the Hōjō have gone. Led by their chieftain Ujimasa, they have emerged as the predominant force in the region. They have even participated in Nobunaga's pacification of Kai and Shimano, working together with his ally Ieyasu to hunt down Shingen's son and successor, Katsuyori. But in the wake of Nobunaga's assassination, sensing an opportunity to expand their territories, they begin to make incursions into Kai and Shinano. They are confronted by Ieyasu who, with the help of allied local chieftains, eventually forces them into a settlement whereby they limit their sphere of activities

Hōjō Ujimasa (1538–90) was the 4th chieftain of the Hōjō, the most powerful clan in the Kantō region. Three centuries earlier, another Kantō clan wielded even more power, for their leaders acted as *shikken* or 'regents' of the Kamakura shogunate. They, too, went by the name of Hōjō, reasons for which Ujimasa's clan came to be known as the Later Hōjō.

In 1554, Ujimasa's father, Ujiyasu, signed an alliance with two other local potentates: Takeda Shingen in Kai Province and Imagawa Yoshimoto in Suruga Province. To seal the pact, Ujimasa was made to marry Shingen's daughter, Ōbai, at the age of sixteen. Five years later, Ujiyasu went into retirement and Ujimasa took over the reins from his father.

Ujimasa' first years at the head of his clan were marked by his rivalry with another local potentate: Uesugi Kenshin. Ujimasa's talents were first seriously put to the test In 1561, when Kenshin rallied a large number of Kantō chieftains and marched toward Odawara Castle. Meeting his enemy out in the field, Ujimasa's forces repeatedly clashed with those of Kenshin. When he was finally thrown back on the protection of his castle, he called in the help of his two powerful allies, and Kenshin withdrew empty-handed.

The next challenge to Ujimasa's hegemony in the Kantō region came three years later, when his forces clashed at Kōnodai with those of the Satomi from the Bōsō Peninsula. Persuading a large number of local chieftains to join his cause, Ujimasa initially achieved some victories. But when, on 25 September 1567, he was routed by Satomi Yoshihiro in the Battle of Mifuneyama, Ujimasa lost control over the Bōsō Peninsula.

Meanwhile, Ujimasa's alliance with the Takeda and the Imagawa, too, began to falter. The first seams came undone in 1560, when Imagawa Yoshimoto was slain in the Battle of Okehazama by the upstart warlord Oda Nobunaga. He left behind a heavily weakened clan, a weakness that was exploited by Takeda Shingen when, in 1568, he broke his alliance with the Imagawa and invaded Suruga. Shingen intended to share the spoils with Ujimasa, but despite being married to Shingen's daughter, Ujimasa declined and broke off his alliance with his father-in-law. What followed were several years of hard campaigning, chiefly against Ujimasa'a longstanding enemy Kenshin and his newly gained enemy Shingen.

Takeda Shingen's death in 1573 and Uesugi Kenshin's death in 1578 heralded a decade of unlimited Hōjō expansion in the Kantō, even into their former territory on the Bōsō Peninsula. Ujimasa's free hand was guaranteed by his new alliance with Oda Nobunaga and Tokugawa Ieyasu. As a result, by the end of the 1580s, the Hōjō ruled supreme in much of Izu, Musashi, Shimōsa, Kazusa, Kōzuke, and even parts of Hitachi, Shimotsuke, and Suruga.

to the Kantō. On 30 September 1583, the pact is reinforced by the marriage of Ieyasu's second daughter, Toku-*hime*, to Ujimasa's twenty-one-year-old son, Ujinao. The Hōjō use the truce with Ieyasu to seize yet more territories in the northern Kantō, even after 1587, when Hideyoshi issues an edict (*Sōbu jirei*) forbidding all chieftains in the region from waging war with each other. Assured of their newly won status in the east, they are willing to recognize Hideyoshi as the new hegemon for the rest of Japan, sending their envoy, Kasawara Yasuaki, to Kyoto to convey the message. Hideyoshi, on his part, is also happy with the arrangement, hoping to eventually deal with the Hōjō in the east as he has dealt with the Mōri in the west. But when, the next year, he invites Ujimasa and his son Ujinao to Kyoto to attend the celebration of his successful campaigns against Shikoku and Kyūshū, both men refuse to make their appearance. They should have obliged. Within weeks, Hideyoshi is drafting plans for their punishment.

Frayed relations are again mended by Ieyasu. It is with Ieyasu's help that, in March 1589, Hideyoshi and the Hōjō work out the details of a settlement concerning former Hōjō territories in Kōzuke Province: one-third is to be given to Sanada Masayuki, the lord of Ueda Castle, who captured those territories on behalf of Takeda Katsuyori but has now submitted to Hideyoshi's rule. His eastern stronghold of Numata Castle, however, situated at the center of the province, is to be ceded to the Hōjō, along with a generous two-thirds of his former territories east of the Tone River. In return, he is given Minowa Castle, some twenty miles south of Numata. For half a year the new boundaries are respected. Ujimasa even promises to come up to the capital to meet Hideyoshi. But toward the end of November, he instead orders Inomata Kuninori, the new keeper of Numata Castle, to capture neighboring Nagurumi Castle. That castle stands on the opposite west bank of the Tone River, firmly in the newly recognized Sanada territory.

By this point, Hideyoshi has lost his last scraps of patience with the Hōjō. Informed through Ieyasu of their latest actions, he send envoys toward their headquarters of Odawara Castle with a stark message:

> Having received Ujimasa's assurance that he intended to come up to the capital, Lord Hideyoshi was inclined to pardon his indiscretions.

Indeed, he has granted the Hōjō most of the Sanada territories in Kōzuke. However, the recent assault on Nagurumi Castle is a betrayal that upsets Lord Hideyoshi's rulings and is unforgivable.

Hideyoshi demands that those involved in the attack on Nagurumi Castle be handed over and punished. Ujimasa and his son refuse. It wasn't on their orders, they claim, that the castle was captured; the castle's keeper has simply gone over to their side of his own free volition. Why, then, would they need to attack a castle that was handed over freely in the first place? Their excuses do not wash with Hideyoshi, nor with Ieyasu, who has told him otherwise. The castle's keeper, Suzuki Shigenori, has done no such thing. It was one of his retainers, a traitor by the name of Nakayama Kurōemon, who lured his master away under false pretenses and thus helped Inomata Kuninori capture the stronghold. In reward, the Hōjō have now made Kurōemon the new master of Nagurumi Castle. Ieyasu's version of events is underscored by the actions of another Hōjō vassal, Fujita Uikuni, the master of nearby Hachigata Castle, who copies Kuninori's example and makes incursions into the territories of Utsunomiya Kunitsuna.

Ujimasa and Ujinao lay siege to Utsunomiya castle

Hideyoshi's Jurakudai Palace in Kyoto

On the last day of December, Hideyoshi sends word to Ieyasu to prepare for a campaign against the Hōjō at Odawara Castle next spring and to come and visit him in Kyoto to work out the details. By now, Ieyasu has also had enough of the Hōjō and their shenanigans. Early in January 1590, he breaks off all ties with the husband and stepfather of his daughter and sets out from his headquarters of Hamamatsu Castle toward the capital. Meeting with Hideyoshi at his opulent Jurakudai palace, he concurs that they should punish the Hōjō—that they should launch a vast campaign that encompasses the whole of the Kantō region. Only then will the region know peace.

By this time, Hideyoshi has already sent the Hōjō a formal declaration of war. Equally issued on the last day of December (24 November by the Lunisolar calendar) Hideyoshi legitimizes his move by claiming to act on behalf of none other than the emperor himself. Part of the long text reads:

> In recent years the Hōjō have scorned our imperial government, have failed to come up to the capital, and, above all, have followed their own obstinate ways, thereby throwing the Kantō region into utter disarray…in doing so, they have disobeyed the commandments of

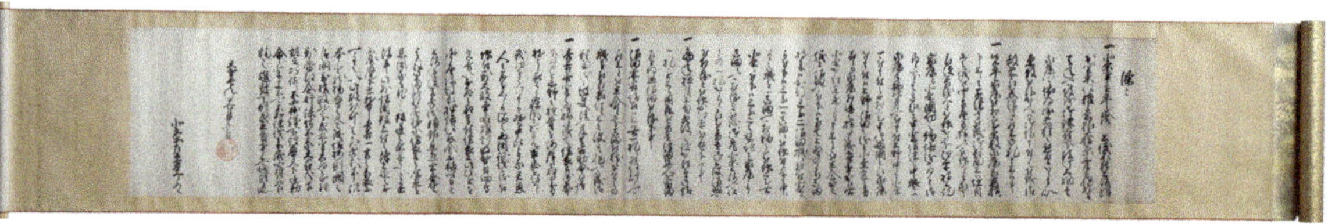

The full text of Hideyoshi's declaration of war against the Hōjō

heaven and plotted against the imperial capital, and thus they shall undergo divine punishment.

Though the emperor has given no such sanction, letters with the same gist are sent to a large number of other powerful chieftains in the region, not only to enlist their support but also to put them on notice in case they might want to contemplate copying the Hōjō example.

The strategy Hideyoshi and Ieyasu eventually work out consists of two phases: it starts with a vast field campaign to reduce the Hōjō's numerous satellite castles, followed by the actual siege of their headquarters or *honjō* of Odawara Castle. The first phase is a multi-pronged one: Hideyoshi and Ieyasu are to move the bulk of their forces up the Tōkaidō toward the Hakone Pass. Meanwhile, along the Nakasendō, a host of allied chieftains are to lead their armies toward the Usui Pass to tackle the many Hōjō's satellite castles in the Kantō plain. The third prong of the attack is over water. For this, Hideyoshi has enlisted the support of Mōri Terumoto, whose armies Hideyoshi faced at Takamatsu Castle eight years earlier. Once the Hōjō's outer defenses have been destroyed, the three forces are to converge on Odawara Castle, with some luck at roughly the same time.

A vast army is required to carry out this plan, hundreds of thousands of men. All the chieftains and their armies in Japan's pacified isles are to contribute to this campaign, none excluded. They are to contribute men according to the rice yields of their territories. More than fifty of Japan's influential chieftains eventually participate in Hideyoshi's venture. Thirty of them make up the main force that is to move toward Odawara along the Tōkaidō under the command of Hideyoshi and Ieyasu. Among them are men like Kuroda Yoshitaka, who played such an important role in Hideyoshi's campaign to subdue western Honshu. The same is true for men like

Sakawa R.
Mt. Fuji
Tokaidō
Odawara
Yamanaka
Sanmaibashi
SAGAMI
SURUGA
Nirayama
BAY
IZU
BAY
PEN.
Shimoda

末廣五十三次
小田原

Odawara Castle, the headquarters of the Hōjō clan

Hosokawa Tadaoki, Ukita Hideie, and Asano Nagamasa. Their total number of men is close to one hundred and seventy thousand. The force that is to descend on the Kantō from the interior along the Nakasendō is smaller but still impressive: some thirty-five thousand men. They are led by Maeda Toshiie, an old Nobunaga stalwart; and Uesugi Kagekatsu, who, unlike his father, has aligned himself with Hideyoshi. The sea-borne force is largely made up of Mōri men, though there are also a substantial number of Chōsokabe and other clans with a naval tradition. Finally, there are also a number of local Kantō clans—the Satake, the Utsunomiya, the Yūki, and the Satomi—who in effect comprise a fourth column.

The Hōjō, meanwhile, are also mobilizing. They requisition all the able-bodied men between the ages of fifteen and seventy from all the villages under their control to report for duty at one of their many satellite castles in the Kantō region. Drawn from poor villages and fighting on meager rations, they are not the most motivated of warriors. And thus their womenfolk and children are required to report along with them at the castle in question, where they are then placed in a dedicated turret as hostages to ensure their menfolk put up a good fight. To provide them with the kind of firepower to repel the attackers, many of the heavy bronze bells that have sounded the hour at the Kantō's many temples are molten down to cast cannon.

On 24 February 1590, three months after Hideyoshi issued his declaration of war, the Hōjō leaders convene a war council at their *goten* within the inner citadel of Odawara Castle. All clansmen of note are present to decide the strategy they are to pursue in the face of Hideyoshi's approaching army: are they to come out fighting, or are they to barricade themselves in at Odawara? Ujiteru and Ujikuni want to come out fighting. Especially Ujikuni, the youngest of the five Hōjō brothers, is vehemently opposed to letting themselves be trapped in their headquarters. He passionately argues that they need to face Hideyoshi's forces out in the field, and not even in their own territory, but along Fuji River, west of the Hakone Pass, both great natural barriers that will work in their favor. Ujinori, the oldest of the five, whose stronghold of Yamanaka Castle guards the Hakone Pass, disagrees. He argues that they should rely on the combined strength of their strongholds, only in that way will they be able to withstand Hideyoshi's huge army, which outnumbers them four to one. Ujimasa concurs, and after more heated arguing it is decided that they are to entrench themselves in their strongholds as best they can.

Hideyoshi and Ieyasu arrive at Sanmaibashi Castle in Numazu on the first of May 1590. Built by the Imagawa, the small castle stands on the western foot of the Izu Peninsula. To reach Odawara Castle they still have to cross the Hakone Pass. Their first obstacle toward the pass is Yamanaka Castle. Its name, 'Among the Mountains,' says it all. Built a few decades earlier by Ujimasa's father, Ujiyasu, it sits halfway the long road up the western slope toward the pass and is made up of a succession of baileys that ascend the slope like a giant flight of stairs. The lowest and at the same time most formidable bailey is the Daisaki-*demaru*, an outlying barbican that has only recently been refashioned by Ujimasa to withstand Hideyoshi's assault.

The siege of Yamanaka Castle is led by Hideyoshi's twenty-two-year-old son Hidetsugu, assisted by a left flank under the command of Ieyasu and a right flank led by Ikeda Terumasa. Their combined force is more than a hundred thousand men. Ensconced within the castle are no more than four thousand. The castle's fall seems a forgone conclusion. It is not. When, early

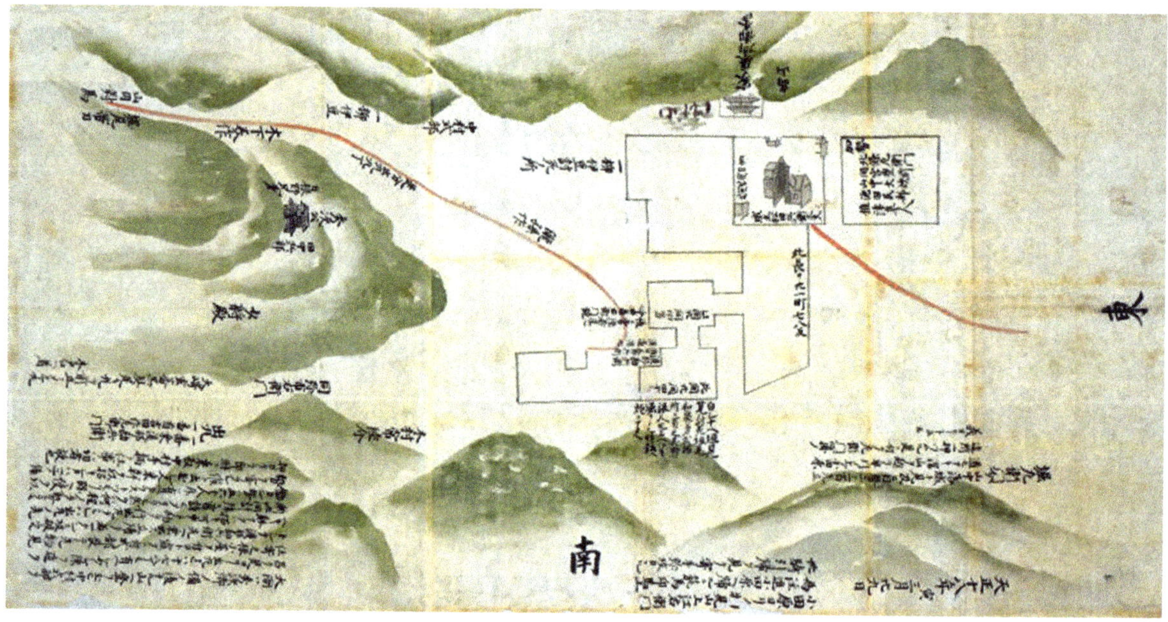

Contemporary map of Yamanaka Castle along the Tōkaidō

in the morning of 3 May, Hidetsugu wrongheadedly orders his men to take the castle by force and storm the Daisaki-*maru* they are met with heavy fire from a large unit of *teppō ashigaru* under the command of the seventy-two-year-old veteran Mamiya Yasutoshi.

Meanwhile, Ieyasu, who has taken charge of the assault on the stronghold's west bailey, also has a hard time of it. His men manage to advance toward the inner citadel, but then run into trouble when they have to negotiate the treacherous *shōji-bori*, a maze of man-deep dry moats whose floors are covered by a checkered pattern of ridges that impede both forward and sideway progress. When they finally breach the inner citadel, its last defenders ensconce themselves in wooden turrets and continue to offer fierce resistance. In the end, they storm the towers too, but again at the cost of countless casualties. The *Watanabe Suian oboe-gaki* describes the final dramatic stages of the siege:

> The hundred or so officers and men who defended each turret were eventually overcome by a billowing wave of advancing troops so that, one by one, they and their assailants crashed into the moats below along with the turrets.

By the end of the day, Yamanaka Castle has fallen. But Hidetsugu's insistence on a quick, forced siege has cost his men dearly. Casualties are especially high at the Daisaki-*maru*. Scores of Hidetsugu's men find their end below the barbican's steep ramparts. Among them is Hitotsuyanagi Naosue, who has served Hideyoshi for more than twenty years. He belongs to the famed Kiboro-*shū*, Hideyoshi's elite horse guard. Hearing the news of Naosue's death, the otherwise so detached Hideyoshi is overcome by a sudden depression and is unable to speak for three days.

By the time Hideyoshi rides down into Yumoto, on 8 May, his mood has lifted. The five days in the fresh spring mountain air have reinvigorated him. He takes up residence at the Sōun Temple, the ancestral temple of the Hōjō, and sends for his womenfolk to join him. There is much at Yumoto to divert them. Known for its hot springs it is a popular destination for those who want to enjoy a restorative bath. He also invites many of his high-society

The **Kiboro-shū** was Hideyoshi's elite guard, which was handpicked by the *taikō* himself. They were selected from the Shichite-*gumi* (see note in the chapter on the siege of Ōsaka Castle), the wider guard of the House of Toyotomi, which not only escorted the *taikō* during his campaigns in the field but also served as guards at his castles of residence. Whereas the Shichite-*gumi* numbered in the thousands, the Kiboro-*shū* consisted of two dozen men. The elite guard derived its name from the yellow, balloon-like capes (*horo*) its members were allowed to wear on their backs during the so-called *musha-zoroe*, the 'general assembly of warriors.' An even more select guard was the Akaboro-*shū*, which consisted of just four members, were allowed to wear crimson (*aka*) capes. Both units had their origin in the black and crimson guards (also known as the Order of the Black and Red Mantel) of Oda Nobunaga, which were selected from among his pages and horse guard.

The somewhat odd-looking cape had its origin in Japan's early medieval times, in the heyday of the bow and arrow. Worn on the back of a warrior's armor, the cape was deemed a good way of protecting against enemy arrows, or at least to dampen their impact, thus reducing the risk of a mortal wound, especially when a warrior was on the move, and the wind caused it to bulge. Later, during the Muromachi period, to increase the cape's effectiveness, it was draped over a bamboo structure, not unlike a large carpet beater. With time—especially after the introduction of firearms—they became one of a warrior's wider paraphernalia heraldry, along with the *sashimono* or 'banner' and the *fukinuki* or 'hollow streamer.'

A member of Nobunaga's Akaboro-shū

acquaintances, celebrities from Kyoto society, to come and entertain him and the high-ranking commanders who visit his headquarters on a daily basis to report on developments in the field. Among his illustrious guests are men like Hon-inbō Sansa, one of the country's best Go players. Or Hon'ami Kōetsu, a man who started out as a sword polisher but has climbed the social ladder through his mastery in other fields like calligraphy and painting. His lacquerware and pottery, too, are highly sought after, and many of his creations adorn the shelves of Hideyoshi's teahouses. To enjoy tea and have Kōetsu explain the niceties of his creations, Hideyoshi also invites his master of tea ceremonies Sen no Rikyū to organize a huge tea party.

It is not all fun and play at Yumoto. Whilst enjoying the company of his guests at the Sōun Temple, Hideyoshi regularly rides down to the eastern slope of Mt. Kasagake, less than an hour downhill from Yumoto. There, a workforce of some twenty thousand men under the overall direction of Kuroda Yoshitaka has been put to work to build a full-blown castle, Ishigakiyama, a stronghold replete with stone walls and turrets. A spacious inner citadel is flanked on the east by a second and third bailey and on the west by a small *demaru* or barbican. Much of the forest covering the slope of the mountain has been cleared, but not east of the construction site, in the direction of Odawara Castle—no need, yet, to let the Hōjō know what he is up to.

Down below, in the valley surrounding the Hōjō stronghold, Hideyoshi's forces are beginning to arrive. The men of Ikeda Terumasa, Hori Hidemasa, Hasegawa Hidekazu, and Kimura Shigekore, who have by now recovered from the hard fighting at Yamanaka Castle, have already taken up positions

Yumoto, known for its hot springs

The mighty Sakawa River, with Odawara Castle in the background, and the Hakone Mountains beyond

at the foot of the Hakone Mountains, at the castle's southwest Hakone and Hayakawa entrances, just where the Tōkaidō levels out along the Haya River. Ieyasu, too, has led his men down the Hakone Pass. He has forded the mighty Sakawa River and has set up his headquarters on its north bank, opposite the castle's northeast Sannō, Shibutori, and Isaida entrances. The gap between him and Hideyoshi at Yumoto is filled by the latter's son, Hidetsugu, who takes up position opposite the castle's northwest Kuno and Ogikubo entrances.

The circle is closed by a vast fleet under the command of Chōsokabe Motochika. The fleet is largely made up of Mōri ships of war, which sailed from Hiroshima at the end of February and have arrived in Suruga Bay on 1 April. By the end of the month, the fleet has been augmented by vessels sent by other naval chieftains, causing it to swell to an armada of well over a thousand ships. With these, they attack Shimoda Castle, on the southern tip of the Izu Peninsula, the headquarters of the Hōjō fleet.

Some twenty thousand warriors land on the peninsula's southern tip and make their way toward the castle. But halfway, on 29 April, when they reach the vicinity of the Iwadono Temple, they are intercepted by a force under the command of Shimizu Eikichi. With only a few hundred men, the latter is vastly outnumbered, and he and most of his men are killed in action.

Hostilities at the castle commence on 4 May. For the next three weeks, Eikichi's older brother, Yasuhide, continues to offer resistance. But when Motochika orders his men to drag cannon up a nearby hill from where they proceed to bombard the stronghold, its defenders, who are by then only six hundred strong, are obliterated.

Finally, on 26 May, Yasuhide is forced to concede defeat and surrenders the castle. Having taken possession of Shimoda Castle, Motochika orders his fleet to heave anchor and round the peninsula. Toward the end of May, the fleet arrives at the head of Sagami Bay and anchors under the shore at Odawara Castle.

Other commanders take longer to arrive. Hosokawa Tadaoki, Tsutsui Sadatsugu, and Gamō Ujisato, for instance. They have taken part in another siege on the Izu Peninsula, that of Nirayama Castle, some ten miles south of Yamanaka Castle. Yet their men are still fresh, for the castle has been taken without much fighting. The siege has been led by Oda Nobukatsu, who wisely opted for a less aggressive approach than Hidenaga at Yamanaka Castle. For more than four months the castle's defenders, led by Hōjō Ujinori, have held out. Only once is the standoff broken. Responsible is Ogasawara Tanba, the man appointed chief negotiator but who grows so frustrated with the endless rounds of talks that he ignores Nobukatsu's orders and leads his men in a surprise assault on the stronghold. He pays for it with his life. Negotiations are taken over by the more levelheaded Kuroda Yoshitaka, and finally, on 25 June, Ujinori agrees to surrender his castle.

The main reason that has led Ujinori to his decision is news of the fate of the other Hōjō satellite castles in the Kantō region. During the four months that his castle has been under siege, one castle after another has fallen before the onslaught of the huge force that has descended on the Kantō from the interior under the overall command of Maeda Toshiie and Uesugi Kagekatsu.

On 2 May, the armies of the two chieftains have met up just east of the Usui Pass to lay siege to Matsuida Castle, the Hōjō's westernmost stronghold in the Kantō. On 23 May, after less than a month, the stronghold falls after its master, Daidōji Masashige, has defended his castle with everything at his disposal. It is still woefully inadequate. Most of his more able-bodied men have been ordered to help in the defense of Odawara Castle. What he is left with is a skeleton force of just a few hundred men, most of them advanced in age or with little fighting experience and armed with poor equipment. It is an ailment that is symptomatic of garrisons of most of the smaller strongholds in the region. Miyazaki, Sho, Maebashi, Minowa, Shiroi, Matsuyama, Nitta Kanayama, Ōgo, and Niibari—all of them succumb within a matter of weeks if not days. Their fall is hastened by none other than Daidōji Masashige, who has negotiated favorable conditions for surrender for his kin and subjects. In return, he is now using his extensive knowledge of the terrain and each castle's weaknesses to give Hideyoshi's army the advantage.

It is exactly there where the castle garrisons are strong, well equipped, and well rationed that Hideyoshi's juggernaut stalls. At Hachigata Castle, for instance, some thirty miles farther east along the Nakasendō. It is defended by Hōjō Ujikuni. Ujikuni, who had argued so hard with his brothers at their war council at Odawara two months earlier, has refused to follow Ujimasa's lead. Instead of contributing his best men to the defense of Odawara Castle, he has led them back to his stronghold. Yet there are only three thousand of them—less than a tenth of the army they face—and thus he has no other option than to ensconce himself in his stronghold in the hope that Odawara survives. Perhaps then they can mount a counterattack.

It is as if Hideyoshi senses the danger that Ujikuni's young and spirited resistance poses. From his new headquarters at Yumoto, he orders his brother-in-law Asano Nagamasa to rapidly lead an army of twenty thousand men northward to help in the siege of Hachigata Castle—Odawara Castle might be surrounded but they need the Maeda and Uesugi forces to make it fall.

Nagamasa, one of Hideyoshi's Five Commissioners, is an excellent commander, who has already contributed greatly to the campaigns to pacify Chūgoku and Kyūshū. Yet he also has a mind of his own. No sooner has he departed than he begins to attack other castles along the way. The first is

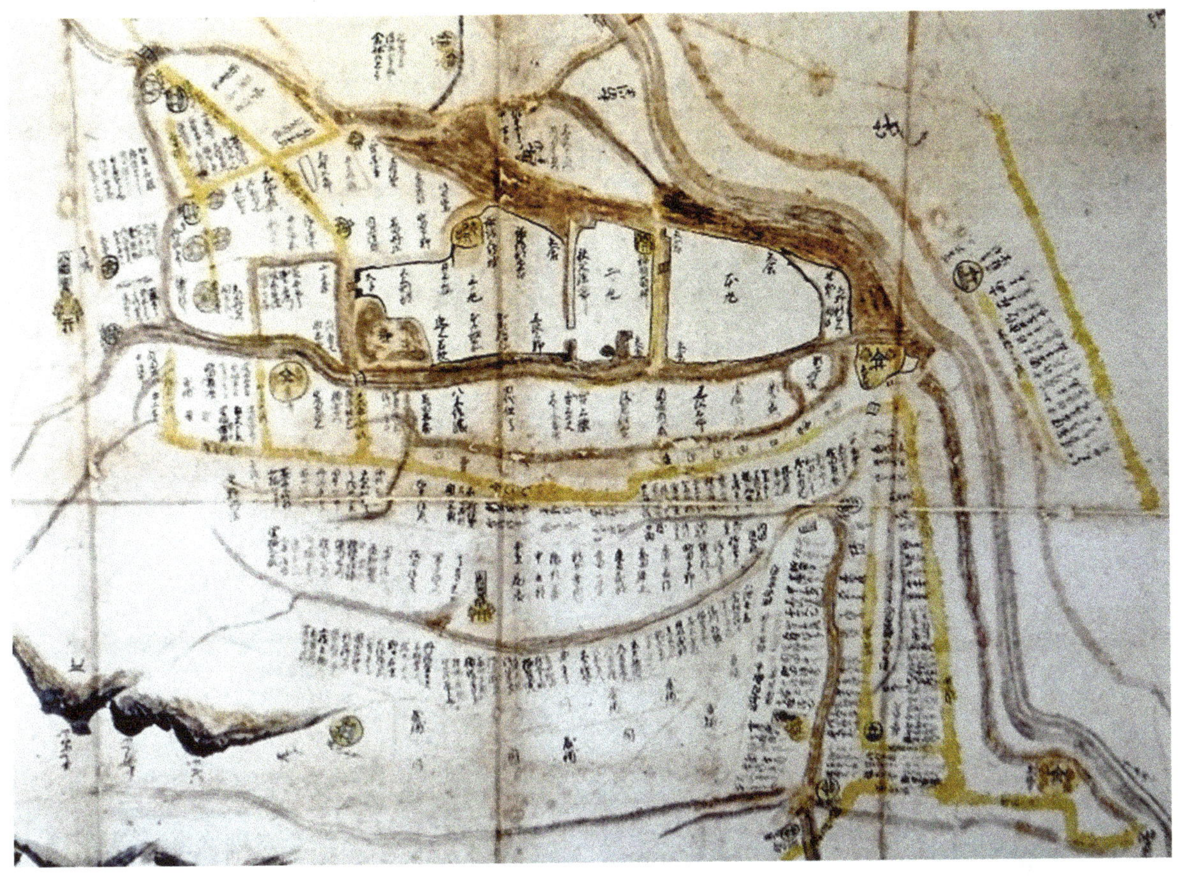

Contemporary map of the siege of Hachigata Castle

Tamanawa Castle, which falls on 25 May. Then follows Edo Castle, which opens its gates a week later. Other castles follow in rapid succession: Edosaki, on 6 June; Usui, on 12 June; and Motosakura, on 19 June. In all, a staggering twenty-six castles have been captured by Nagamasa by the time he reaches the vicinity of Saitama and lays siege to Iwatsuki Castle, some thirty miles east of Hachigata.

Hideyoshi, however, is distinctly underwhelmed. Capturing castles that offer practically no resistance, in his view, does not amount to meritorious service. On the contrary, Nagamasa's actions go directly against his orders to lead his men in a forced march northward to help in the siege of Hachigata Castle. He has already reminded Nagamasa of his original brief in a sealed letter on 13 June. To reinforce that message, he sends Nagamasa another

Contemporary map of Iwatsuki Castle

long letter on 21 June, reprimanding him for wasting his time and huge army in reducing insignificant strongholds. He is to capture Iwatsuki Castle by the fastest possible means and proceed to move his troops west to assist Maeda Toshiie and Uesugi Kagekatsu in the siege of Hachigata Castle. As for the surviving defenders, all men alive are to be put to the sword, while the women and children are to be brought to him at Odawara.

By the time Hideyoshi's second letter reaches Nagamasa, Iwatsuki Castle is already on the brink of defeat. To hasten its fall, he changes his strategy

KŌZUKE
Nagurumi
Numata
Maeda
Minowa
SHIMOTSUKE
Kanuma
Matsuida
SHINANO
KANTO
Nakasendō
Hachigata
Oshi
L. Suwa
Matsuyama
Iwatsuki
MUSASHI
Kawagoe
Edo
Edo
Hachiōji
KAI
SAGAMI
EDO
BAY
Mt. Fuji
Tamanawa
Odawara
SURUGA
Yamanaka
Sanmaibashi
SAGAMI
Nirayama
BAY
Sunpu
SURUGA
BAY
Tōkaidō
Shimoda

from simple encirclement to one of attack, setting fire to most of its buildings and launching a massive assault with the full force of his twenty-thousand men. Two days later, on 23 June, Iwatsuki Castle falls. More than a thousand of its defenders have perished in the withering assault. But, to his great credit, Nagamasa ignores Hideyoshi's instructions to put the survivors to the sword. There are practically no warriors left to put to the sword, most of the survivors being non-combatants. He is put into a more difficult position with respect to their leaders, who are in fact two women. One is Chōrin'in, who is none other than Hōjō Ujimasa's indomitable younger sister. She is the wife of Ōta Ujisuke, the former lord of Iwatsuki Castle. The other woman warrior is the young Koshōshō, who is married to Ōta Ujifusa, the castle's present lord, who has been called upon to help in the defense of Odawara Castle. Since there is no one left in the castle to take care of them, he entrusts them to Ishimaki Yasumasa, a former Hōjō vassal who has been captured and detained at Suruga but is released to take care of the women.

Nagamasa Joins Maeda Toshiie and Uesugi Kagekatsu at Hachigata Castle a few days later. Together, it takes them three more weeks to force its lord Ujikuni to surrender. He does so on the condition that his men are spared. He too is left alive on the condition that he take the tonsure and withdraws to the Seiryū Temple, his clan's family temple on the opposite bank of the Arakawa River.

Again Hideyoshi sends Nagamasa instructions, this time to assist Ishida Mitsunari in the siege of Oshi Castle, which is situated roughly halfway between Hachigata and Iwatsuki Castle. The relative ease with which Nagamasa can move his troops around between the Hōjō strongholds is symptomatic of the passive stance they have taken in the conflict. Only rarely does a besieged chieftain sally forth from his stronghold to meet him out in the field.

Oshi Castle poses an even greater challenge than the previous two strongholds, for it is entirely surrounded by water and marshes. It has no clearly defined inner citadel and outer baileys but is rather a cluster of fragmented islands set amid a lake fed by various rivers. The islands are outwardly fortified by raised walls with parapets and palisades, which are interconnected by narrow pathways, while the stronghold's main approaches run through boggy marshes.

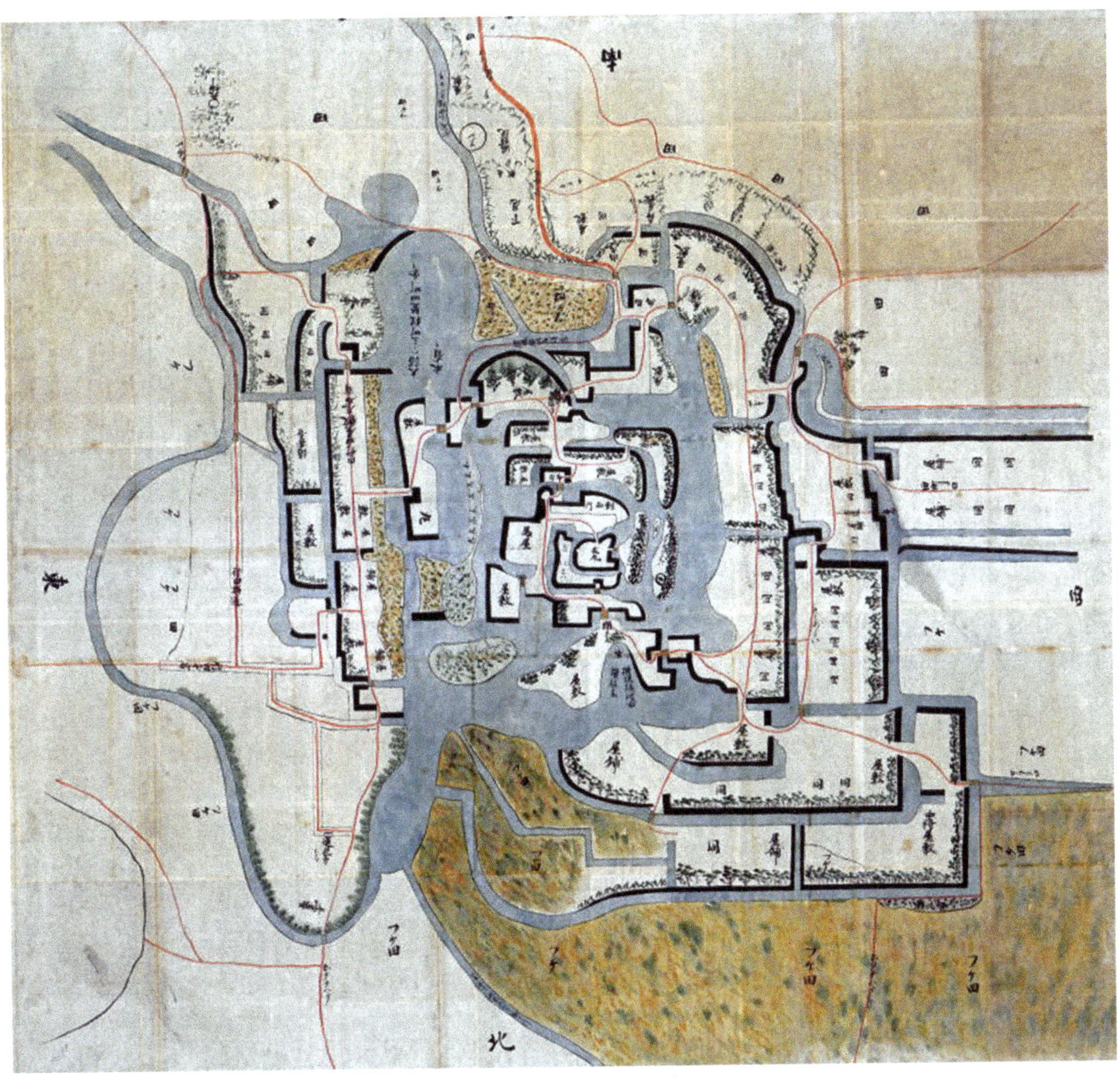

Contemporary map of Oshi Castle

Oshi Castle is the stronghold of Narita Ujinaga, who like many of the other local chieftains, has left for Odawara. He has left his castle under the control of the seventy-four-year-old Narita Yasusue, a man who had already retired to monastic life, but now takes on the heavy duty of facing off a huge army. But on 8 July, just two days after Mitsunari has laid siege to the castle, he passes away. Command is taken over by his son, Nagachika, and it is under his spirited leadership that the castle's three thousand defenders repel one attack after the other.

Hearing of Oshi Castle's resistance, Hideyoshi urges Mitsunari to apply the same strategy by which he has reduced the water-locked stronghold of Takamatsu Castle in Bitchū: by water. And thus Mitsunari orders his men to raise a 20-mile-long crescent-shaped dam, stretching all the way from Kumagaya to Shirakawado, thereby blocking the course of the many rivers and rivulets that feed the vast marshes around the castle. The dam is completed by the middle of July, by which time the rainy season has started, causing the waters to rise so dramatically that even the castle's inner citadel is threatened to be flooded. To avert disaster, its defenders send out a nightly force, which breaches the dam at two locations. It is a brilliant counterattack, for now the water turns itself against the attackers, who are encamped immediately behind the dam. Some 270 of Mitsunari's men die that night.

Over the next few weeks, more forces join those of Mitsunari. By the beginning of August some fifty thousand of Hideyoshi's men are solely engaged in the siege of Oshi Castle—a quarter of those converged on Odawara.

At Odawara, meanwhile, the mood has turned merry. The vast army that has converged around the castle is getting tired of all the waiting. Before long the typical hallmarks of a drawn-out siege begin to manifest themselves: gambling, prostitution, drunken brawls. There are even some desertions, if only out of sheer boredom.

On Hideyoshi's strict orders there are no major assaults on the Hōjō stronghold; it would simply cause too many casualties. Odawara Castle is one of the strongest bastions in the realm. Situated on the east slope of Hachiman Hill, the stronghold was built during the early 13th century by Dohi Tōhira. Yet it is under the powerful and wealthy Hōjō that the stronghold has undergone a number of large-scale expansions. One of them is the addition of a wide third bailey with an outer moat that has swallowed up much of the original castle town in favor of the *buke yashiki* of the Hōjō retainers. A narrow moat that previously dissected the citadel has been widened to create a second bailey that, like the third, surrounds the inner citadel on the north, east, and west.

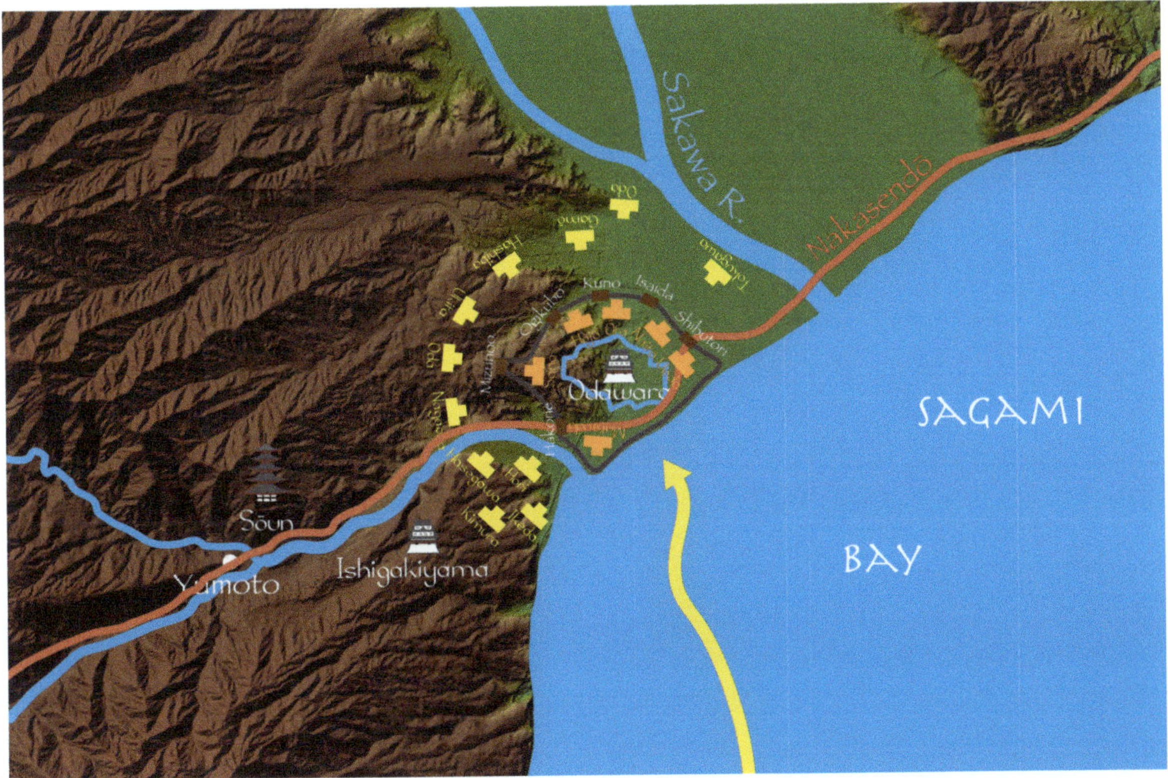

There are some flashes of action. One comes on 23 July, when Ii Naomasa leads his men in a midnight attack on the Sasa-*kuruwa*, a makeshift bailey on the castle's northeast perimeter, and manages to occupy it. It is answered on the first night of August, when Hirosawa Shigenobu assembles a large group of mounted warriors at the castle's Kuno gate from where they launch a surprise attack on the armies of Gamō Ujisato and Seki Kazumasa on the banks of the Sanno River, just north of the castle town. Yet while it produces the spectacle of man-to-man combat between Shigenobu and Ujisato on horseback, it yields no results whatsoever.

The occasional outbreaks provide only a small morale boost to the frustrated and bored warriors inside the stronghold. Though the castle's storehouses and armories are well stocked, the warriors manning the castle's defenses become restless and before long they even begin fighting among each other. Some become so frustrated with the Hōjō's passive stance that

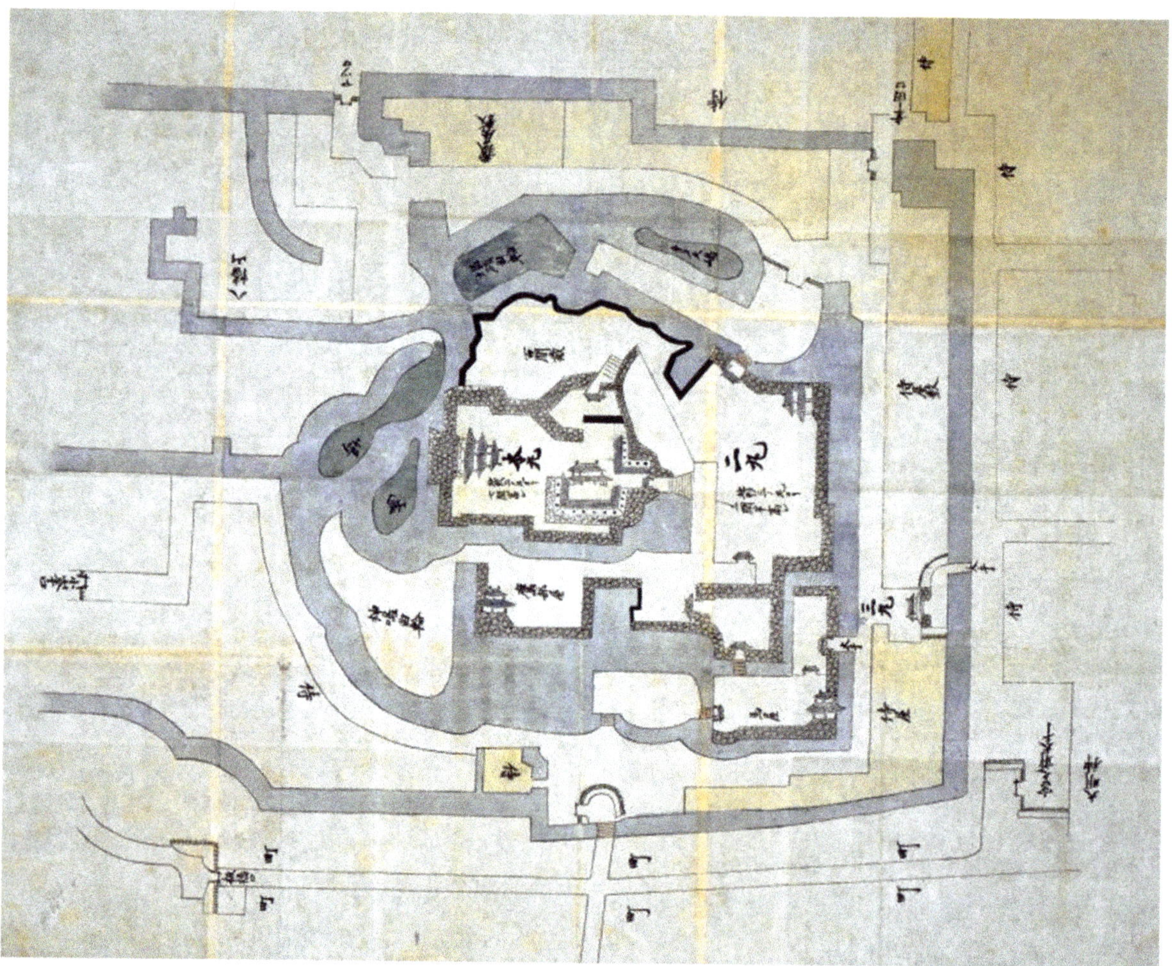

Contemporary map of Odawara Castle

they openly mutiny. One of them is Minagawa Hiroteru, who is charged with the defense of the Takeura Gate. On the night of 11 May, he secretly steals away and rides into Ieyasu's camp to surrender. The Hōjō leaders desperately try to keep their men in check with rounds of disciplinary action, but even they are beginning to despair. As the inevitable begins to impress itself on them, their councils, or *hyōjō*, with their chief retainers, which are traditionally held twice a month, are now held on an almost daily basis. Some even drag on for several days without their members reaching any agreement.

While their meetings drag on, the morale among the Hōjō leaders is undermined by one bad piece of news after the other. It begins with the news, early in May, that Yamanaka Castle has fallen. It is followed by a string of ominous tidings about the rampage of Asano Nagamasa, who seems to be able to capture one castle after another without any serious opposition. Then comes the news, early in June, that, urged by the same Nagamasa, Date Masamune, one of their most powerful allies in the north, has gone over to Hideyoshi's side. Toward the end of June, word reaches Odawara that Iwatsuki and Hachigata castles, their northernmost strongholds in the Kantō, have also been lost. Oshi Castle still seems to be holding out. So is Hachiōji Castle, in the western corner of the Kantō and which controls the Kōshū Kaidō, the highroad into Kai Province. That last glimmer of hope is destroyed when, toward the end of July, rumor reaches Odawara that Hachiōji Castle, too, is lost. Its three thousand defenders are said to have put up a

Contemporary map of Hachiōji Castle

good fight, killing as many as a thousand assailants. But facing a force of more than fifteen thousand, they are utterly outnumbered. Finally, after a day of intense fighting, the castle's defenses are breached and those who are not killed by the enemy or their own hand surrender. By then, the senior retainers and womenfolk have withdrawn to the nearby Goshuden Falls, where they commit ritual suicide and let themselves drop down the fall. It is said that the waters downstream turn crimson for three days. The news is especially devastating to Hōjō Ujiteru, the lord of Hachiōji Castle, who has joined his brothers at Odawara. For among the dead are his wife, Hisa, and all his daughters. The fall of the castle is confirmed and brought home in grueling fashion when, a few days later, a large number of his men's heads are put up on spikes outside Odawara Castle's main gates.

The final and ultimate blow to the Hōjō's will to resist comes on 27 July, when, having completed his new castle of Ishigakiyama, Hideyoshi orders his men to fell all the trees east of the new castle. From the keep of Odawara Castle—from where the new stronghold is now clearly visible—it looks as if a new stronghold has risen overnight. It is all the more intimidating as the newly arisen stronghold has been built according to the most modern standards, with thick and steep stone walls topped by multi-storied turrets. It is the final straw; their will is broken.

Three days later, on 4 August, Hōjō Ujinao rides up to Ishigakiyama Castle to offer Hideyoshi Odawara Castle's surrender on the condition that all their men are spared. Hideyoshi accepts. He only demands the heads of Ujimasa and a number of his chief generals and retainers. Being married to Ieyasu's daughter, Ujinao is spared, but only on the condition that he retire from military life. Two weeks later, having witnessed his father's end, Ujinao departs from Odawara Castle with thirty of his retainers. Traveling down to the Ise Peninsula, he enters one of the temples among the vast temple complex atop Mt. Kōya and takes the tonsure under the name of Kenshōsai. The following year, he travels down to Ōsaka Castle where, on 6 October, Hideyoshi formally pardons him and grants him a 10,000-*koku* domain in Kawachi Province (Ōsaka Prefecture). He will never see it. He dies of a sudden illness while still in Ōsaka at the age of 29.

GIFU

The year is 1600. Tokugawa Ieyasu is keenly aware that this might be the year in which he will reach the goal that Nobunaga set out to achieve—to unify the entire country. Standing in his way is an alliance of western warlords that has coalesced around Ishida Mitsunari, a member of the *Go-Bugyō*, the Council of (five) Commissioners called into life by Hideyoshi to ensure he is succeeded by his infant son, Hideyori. The first move of the western alliance against Ieyasu comes on August 30, when some fifty thousand men under the overall command of Ukita Hideie attack Fushimi Castle, one of Ieyasu's strongholds near the capital. The castle falls after ten days of intense fighting in which its keeper, Torii Mototada, and most of his two thousand men lose their lives.

A week later, on September 16, Mitsunari sets out from his headquarters of Sawayama Castle, on the eastern shore of Lake Biwa. From there he leads some thirty thousand men east along the Nakasendō through the Ibuki Mountains, across what was once the Fuwa barrier, the ancient border between eastern and western Japan. Having entered Mino Province, he captures Ōgaki Castle and turns the place into his temporary headquarters. It appears he wants to entrench himself in Mino, possibly to intercept Ieyasu when he moves west along the Tōkaidō. To do so, he will need the cooperation of Nobunaga's grandson Oda Hidenobu, the lord of Gifu Castle. And

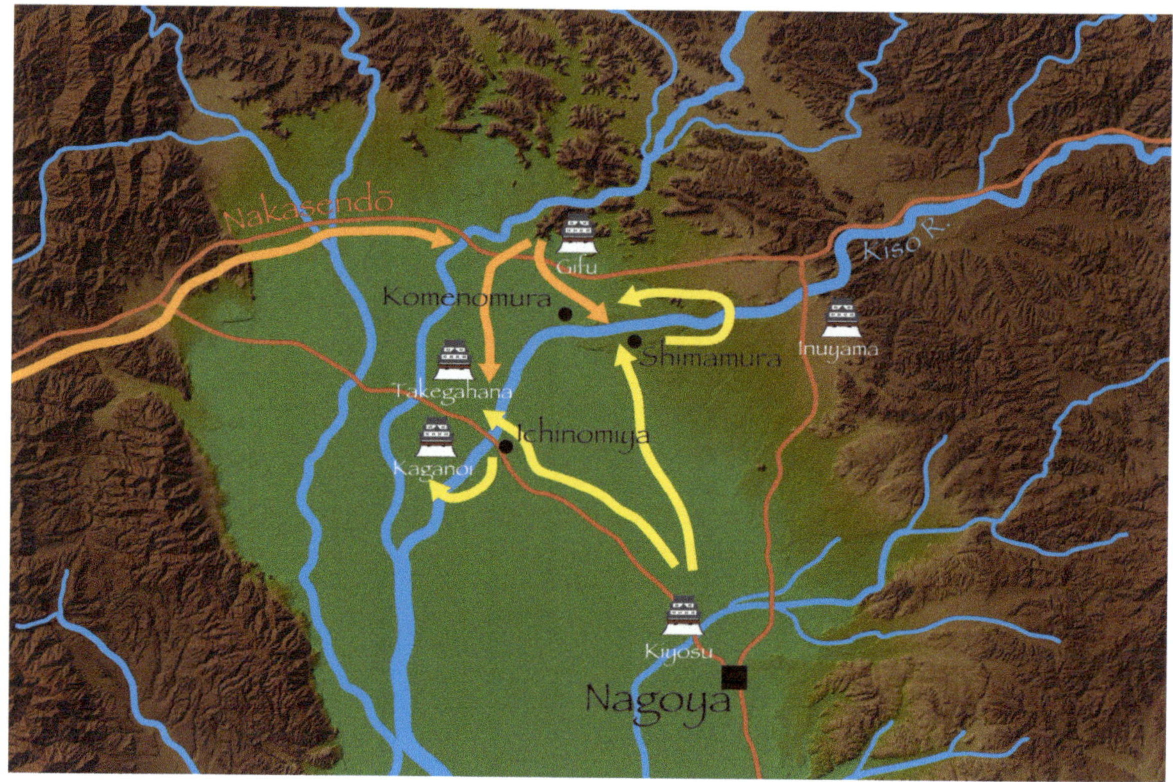

it appears that, in this, he is successful, for not much later, word reaches Ieyasu at Edo Castle that the twenty-year-old Hidenobu has been won over by Mitsunari. It does not surprise Ieyasu. When still an infant by the name of Sanbōshi, Hidenobu had been favored by Hideyoshi to succeed his assassinated grandfather. Ieyasu's eventual succession to that very position has naturally upset the youth, who, despite the political reality, continues to entertain hopes of his clan's restoration to power. Indeed, already a year earlier, when Mitsunari set about reinforcing his stronghold of Sawayama Castle, Hidenobu began doing the same at Gifu.

Ieyasu is not particularly perturbed by the news. Mitsunari's alliance might pose a serious threat; Hidenobu joining them is no more than an added inconvenience. Besides, it will provide a good opportunity to test the cohesion of his own, eastern alliance, which is made up of some two hundred chieftains in all, not all of whom are necessarily staunch supporters of the

Oda Hidenobu (1580–1605) was the oldest son of Oda Nobutada, who in turn was the oldest son of Oda Nobunaga. When both Nobunaga and Nobutada met their end during the Honnō-*ji* Incident (when Akechi Mitsuhide attacked Nobunaga at the Honnō Temple), the two-year-old Hidenobu, who was then still called Sanbōshi, became the play-ball of Nobunaga's top generals who vied for the right to succeed him. The two main players were Toyotomi Hideyoshi and Shibata Katsuie. It was Hideyoshi who took the infant under his wings, promoting him as Nobunaga's legitimate heir, as opposed to Katsuie, who (for similar selfish reasons) supported Nobunaga's third son, Nobutaka. And it was Hideyoshi, in the end, who won through and moved Sanbōshi to Azuchi Castle.

Not long afterward, Sanbōshi's uncle Nobutaka took the boy under his wings and moved him to his headquarters of Gifu Castle. In doing so, he came into conflict with Hideyoshi, who suspected that Nobutaka was moving against him. The standoff came to a head in the winter of 1582, when Hideyoshi mobilized a huge force against Gifu Castle and demanded Sanbōshi be surrendered. Again, Sanbōshi was put up at Azuchi Castle, where he was placed in the custody of Nobunaga's other surviving son, Oda Nobukatsu.

When, in 1588, Sanbōshi came of age and received his formal name of Hidenobu, he did not succeed his grandfather but effectively became one of Hideyoshi's vassal-generals. As such, he took part in the latter's campaign against the Odawara Hōjō, when he was in command of one of Hori Hidemasa's units of *teppō ashigaru*.

It was partly in reward for his contribution to the Odawara campaign, partly to assuage the Oda clan, that, in 1593, Hideyoshi made Hidenobu lord of Gifu Castle with territories in Mino Province to the tune of 130,000 *koku*. During the rest of the 90s, Hidenobu's ties to the house of Toyotomi gradually deepened. He did not directly take part in Hideyoshi's two disastrous campaigns on the Korean Peninsula. Yet he did—along with Hideyoshi's other major allies—make his appearance at Hideyoshi's southern headquarters of Nagoya Castle in Bizen, Kyūshū, when, on 7 July 1594, the *taikō* received a Ming embassy in an initial attempt to negotiate a settlement to the conflict.

Inuyama Castle, situated on the south bank of the Kiso River

Tokugawa cause. That alliance has been split up into two forces: forty thousand men will move toward Inuyama under the command of his son, Hidetada; another thirty thousand men will move toward Kiyosu along the Tōkaidō under his own command. If he can count on the support of the chieftains who have declared themselves on his side, they will be joined along the way by at least the same number.

Meanwhile, a number of his allies have assembled their troops at Kiyosu Castle. Among them are the Yamauchi, the Hosokawa, the Matsushita, the Ii, and the Honda—some seventeen clans in all. Their total number is close to thirty thousand. Their task is to suppress local resistance. Two reliable men are in charge of the operation: Fukushima Masanori and Ikeda Terumasa. The first move comes on 26 September, when the forces of Ii Naomasa and Honda Tadakatsu move their forces northward from Kiyosu to put pressure on Inuyama Castle. Standing on a tall hill on the south bank of the Kiso River, the stronghold guards the border between Owari and Mino. It is controlled by Ishikawa Sadakiyo, who has equally been persuaded by Mitsunari to join his cause. He has been joined by a number of local chieftains, among them Inaba Sadamichi, Katō Sadayasu, Takenaka Shigekado, and Seki Kazumasa.

The same day that Naomasa and Tadakatsu arrive below Inuyama Castle, a missive from Ieyasu in Edo arrives at Kiyosu Castle for the remainder of his forces. He instructs them to move against Oda Hidenobu at Gifu Castle forthwith.

Two days later, on 28 September, Ikeda Terumasa, Asano Yoshinaka, and Yamauchi Kazutoyo lead some eighteen thousand men northward and set up camp at Shimamura, on the south bank of the Kiso River, some ten miles south of Gifu Castle. It is the site of the old Kōda ferry, the place where the Gifu Kaidō crosses the river to connect the Tōkaidō to the Nakasendō at the Ōta post station. At this section, a cluster of small islands sits amid the river, just before it makes a sharp curve southward toward the Bay of Ise.

Facing them on the other side of the river is Oda Hidenobu, who has led half of his nine thousand men toward Komenomura (Kasamatsu). His strategy is to intercept and crush them at the old river crossing. Yet his plan backfires when, early next morning, Terumasa and his men ford the river farther upstream, follow the northern riverbank, and attack Hidenobu's forces on

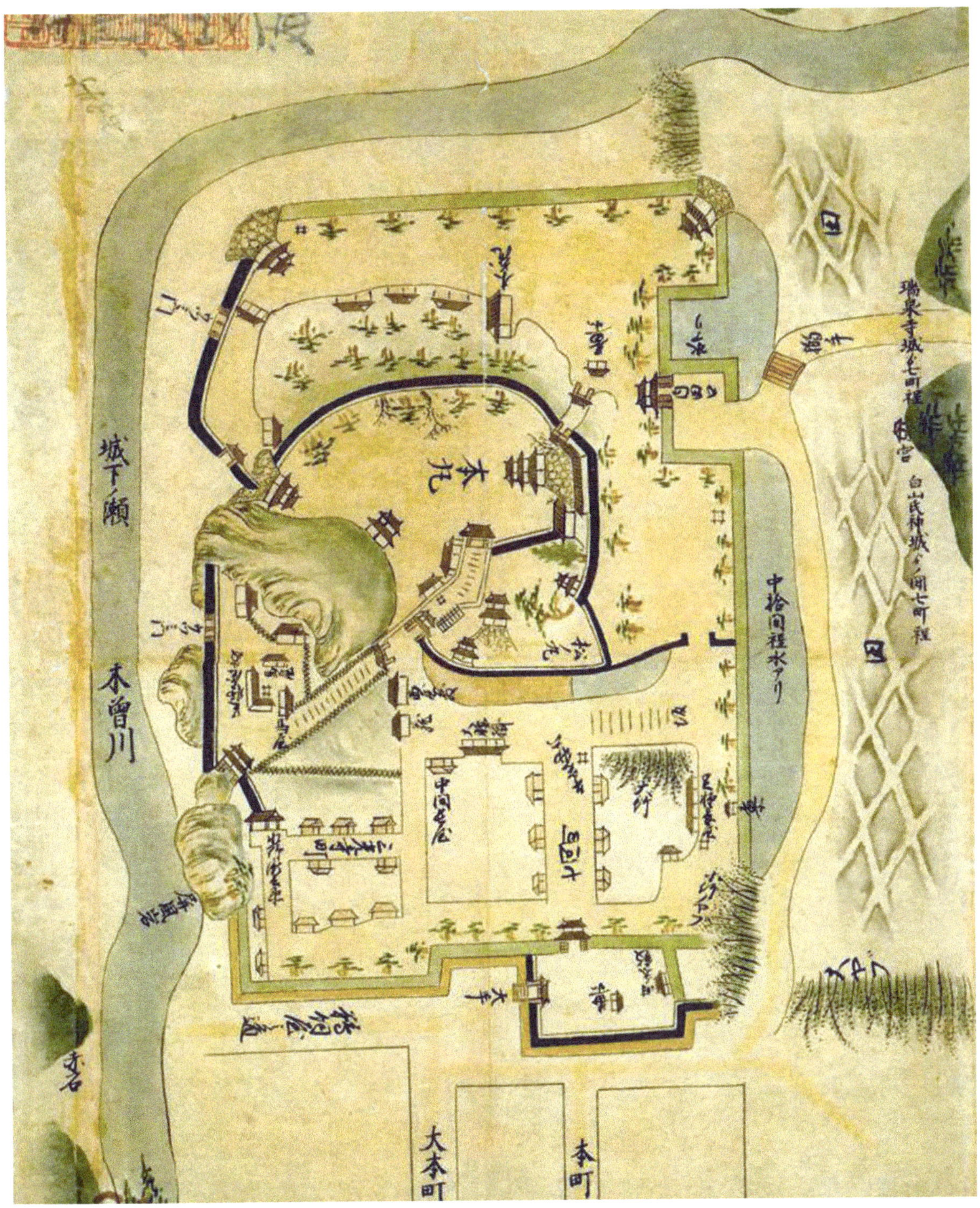

本丸
城下瀬
木曽川
中拾間程水アリ
大手
大本町
本町

The Kōda ferry near Ōta

the flank. They are met by volleys from Hidenobu's *teppō ashigaru*, but it is not enough to force them back across the river. Fighting continues throughout the day. But by the end of the day, it is Hidenobu who is forced to retreat, back to the safety of Gifu Castle.

Meanwhile, some sixteen thousand men under the command of Fukushima Masanori have also kicked into action. Alerted by a signal fire from Terumasa on the morning of 28 September, they try to cross the Kiso River at Ichinomiya, where the Mino Kaidō crosses the river, just south of Komenomura. Yet here they are met by Sugiura Shigekatsu, the lord of Takegahana Castle, whose men are reinforced by warriors from nearby Kaganoi Castle, as well as from Gifu Castle, who fire on Masanori's men from behind palisades along the river bank. To make matters worse, in this section the river is lined by wide and loose sandbanks, making the going particularly tough for Masanori's mounted warriors. And thus he orders his men to retreat. They try again farther downstream the next day. Early that morning, at the hour of the Dragon, using captured boats and hastily assembled rafts, they begin to cross the river south of Kaganoi Castle.

Both armies clash again on the river's west bank, and this time Masanori manages to get all of his men across. Suffering heavy losses, Shigekatsu is forced to fall back to his stronghold of Takegahana Castle before the morning is out. There they entrench themselves as best they can. Shigekatsu and his men ensconce themselves within the inner citadel, while the other forces are dispersed around the castle's second bailey. It seems as if history repeats itself. Sixteen years earlier, Toyotomi Hideyoshi reduced the stronghold by

Contemporary map of the cluster of islands in the Kiso River

building a dam across the nearby Ajika River. Then, those within the castle held out for almost a month. This time around, they last only a day. Late that afternoon, having lost almost all of his men under Masanori's withering attack, Shigekatsu sets fire to his castle and falls on his sword.

Masanori's forces join those of Terumasa along the banks of the Arada River, a tributary to the Nagara River, some five miles southwest of Gifu Castle. From there they split up into seven groups that take up positions at the castle's main approaches: those under the command of Yamauchi Kazutoyo at Shinkanō; those under the command of Arima Toyouji at Nagatsuka;

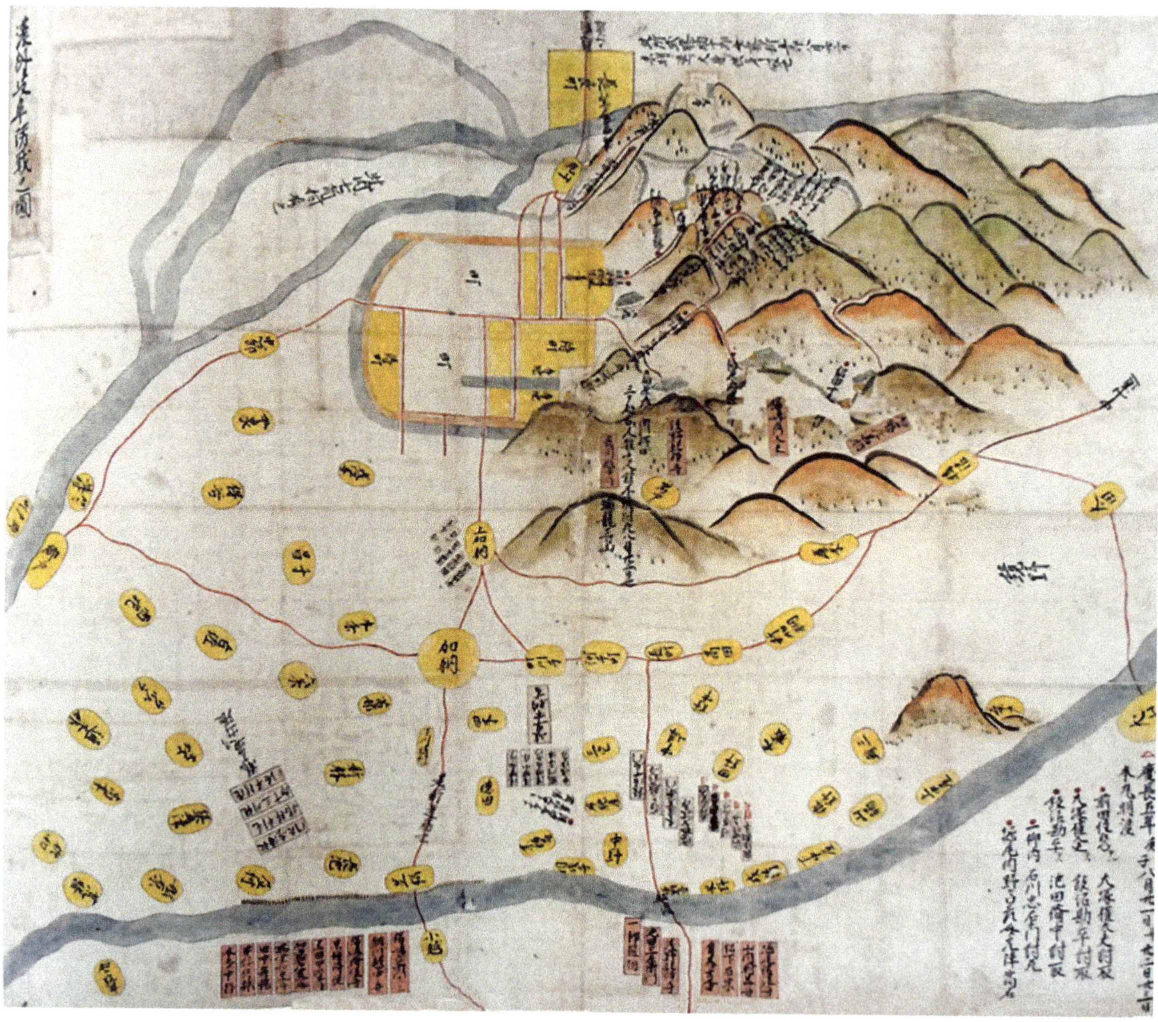

Siege map of Gifu Castle, with the two armies facing each other from across the Kiso River

and those of Horio Tadauji at Furuichiba—the castle's eastern approaches. The remainder, under the command of Kuroda Nagamasa, takes up positions at Kawawatari, the site of the old ferry crossing across the Nagara River immediately west of the castle.

The two commanders face a difficult challenge. Gifu Castle is a mountain stronghold in the best tradition. Sitting atop a ridge along the crest of Mt. Inaba, it commands a sweeping view of the wide stretch of land pincered between the Nagara and Kiso rivers. Captured by Oda Nobunaga in 1567, it has served for almost a decade as his headquarters, a time during which the potentate carried through a number of improvements. Yet it was under his son, Nobutada, who became the castle's master in 1576, that the castle was turned into the most formidable strongholds of its time, with a string of ascending baileys toward an inner citadel crowned with a four-story main keep. All the baileys have been reinforced by high stone walls that are crowned with multi-storied turrets at strategic positions. No one is better aware of the challenge than Ikeda Terumasa. He, after all, had become the lord of Gifu Castle when, in the wake of Nobutada's demise during the Honnō Rebellion, the stronghold was awarded to the Ikeda. He more than anyone knows the castle's strengths. Yet he also is aware of its weaknesses, a knowledge he intends to put to good use during the coming siege.

Inside the castle, Oda Hidenobu holds a heated war council with his senior retainers. Kozukuri Nagamasa, who has argued for Hidenobu to choose Ieyasu's side from the start, believes surrender is the best option. Others are in favor of entrenching themselves as best they can within the castle. Only that way, they argue, can they withstand the onslaught of an army ten times their size, for by now they have lost half their men. But Hidenobu begs to differ. Instead, he orders his men to take up defensive positions in a number of makeshift fortresses they have erected at strategic positions around the castle: one near the Zuiryū Temple, southwest of the castle; one at a crest halfway toward the temple; and one atop Mt. Gongen, well to the east. He himself sets up his headquarters in the castle's inner citadel, from where he sends messengers to Ōgaki and Inuyama castles with urgent requests for reinforcements. With their help, he hopes, they might catch the attacking forces in two pincer movements from the east and from the west.

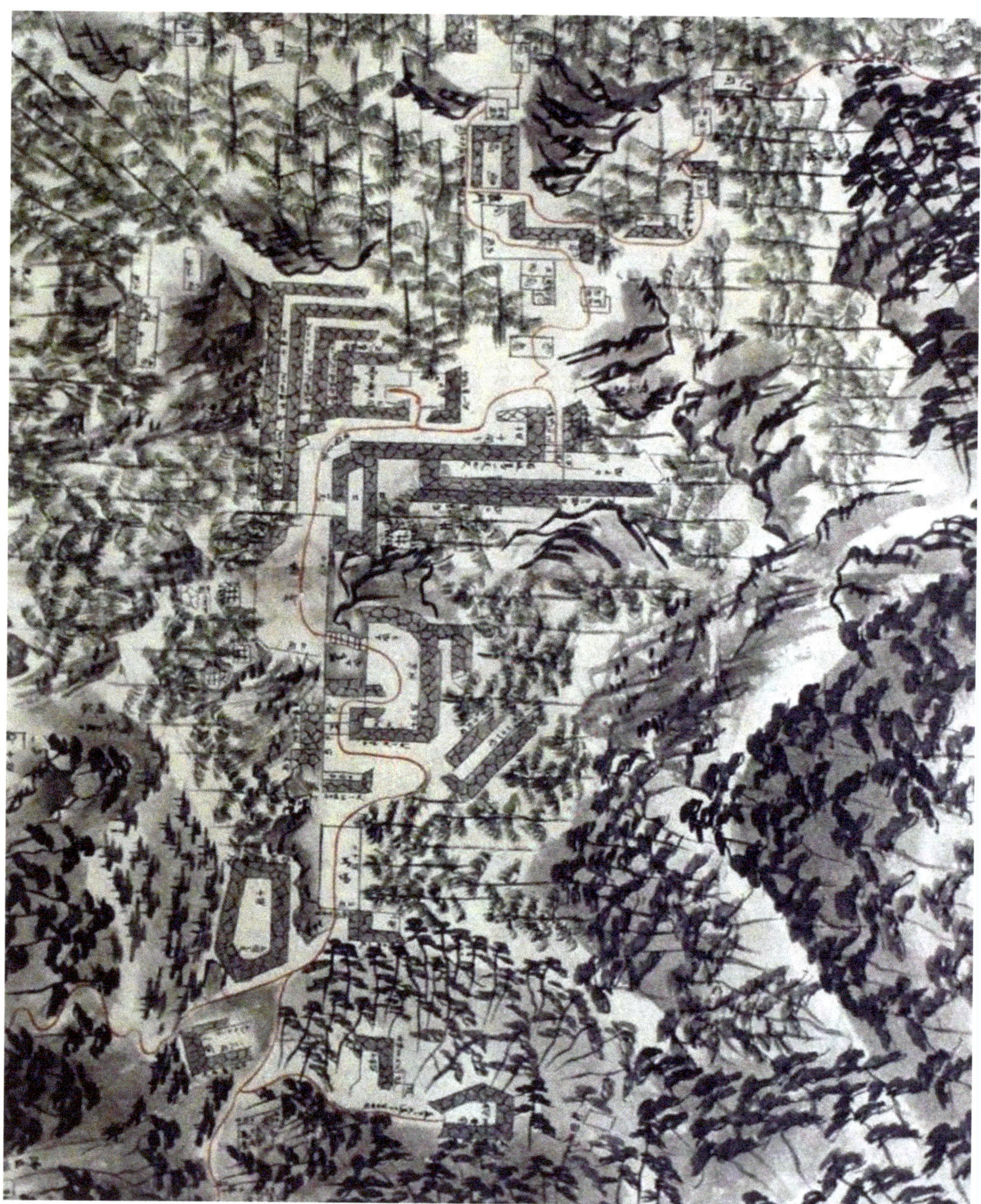

Contemporary map of Gifu Castle and its approaches

Early the next day, 30 September, hostilities open when warriors under the command of Asano Yoshinaga enter the grounds of the Zuiryū Temple and storm the nearby fort. At roughly the same time, forces under the command of Ii Naomasa storm the fortresses atop Mt. Gongen and Mt. Inaba, while Fukushima Masanori and his men try to make their way to the castle's inner citadel. And though the fighting is ferocious, they steadily work their way upward. At one stage, the mountain is rocked when a turret within the second bailey that serves as gunpowder storage catches fire and explodes. By the end of the day, the only part of the stronghold they haven't captured is the inner citadel. There, within the castle's keep, surrounded by his last men, Hidenobu is determined to fight on, hoping that the reinforcements from Inuyama and Ōgaki might still turn the tide in his favor.

But Hidenobu's hopes are in vain; there are no reinforcements. At Inuyama Castle, its lord, Ishikawa Sadakiyo, has been betrayed by his retainers. They have secretly begun negotiations for surrender with Ii Naomasa, agreeing to surrender the castle in return for their lives. One of them, Seki Kazumasa, persuades him to save himself and escape. This he does. Abandoning his stronghold to Naomasa's forces, he makes his way toward Ōgaki Castle, where he joins Mitsunari. The latter, meanwhile, has indeed sent reinforcements toward Gifu Castle, but they have been intercepted and repelled by Kuroda Nagamasa's men while trying to cross the Nagara River at Kawawatari.

It is a hopeless situation and all except Hidenobu realize the game is up. Finally, it is Kozukuri Nagamasa who persuades his young master of the futility of fighting on. And late that night, Hidenobu and the remainder of his men descend Mt. Inaba. From there the defeated lord makes his way to the Entoku-*ji*, the clan's family temple at the mountain's west foot, where he has his head shaved and takes the tonsure. The remainder of his retainers, some thirty-eight men in all, assemble on the porch of the Sōfuku Temple, facing the north bank of the Nagara River. There they collectively cut open their bellies. Their heads are sent to Tokugawa Ieyasu in Edo, who inspects them at Edo Castle and has them interred within the grounds of Edo's Zōjō Temple.

Three weeks after the fall of Gifu Castle, on 21 October, Ieyasu and his eastern forces crush Ishida Mitsunari's alliance on the plains of Sekigahara,

The ceiling of the Sōfuku Temple porch, still stained by the blood of Hidenobu's loyal retainers

some twenty miles west of Gifu Castle. On November 6 of that same year, Mitsunari's head is severed from his body at the capital's Rokujōgawara execution grounds.

ŌSAKA

Following his victory over Mitsunari in the Battle of Sekigahara, Ieyasu sets about to consolidate his position as *Tenka-dono*. In 1603, he moves his headquarters to Edo Castle and establishes the Edo *bakufu* (1603–1867). Then, in the image of the great Minamoto Yoritomo, he has himself appointed *Sei-I Tai Shōgun*, the 'Barbarian Subduing Generalissimo.' At the same time, he abolished the *Go-Tairō*, the Council of Regents put in place by Hideyoshi to safeguard the succession of his son Hideyori. At the same time, he carries through a nationwide redistribution of lands, taking away three-quarters of the territories formerly belonging to Toyotomi vassals. He stops short, however, of dealing with Hideyori himself, a young man to whom many still look up as their true overlord. Instead, he seeks to contain Hideyori and his allies.

Starting in 1601, Ieyasu builds a ring of strongholds in the Home Province and the Kantō region. Meanwhile, he sets about on the large-scale reconstruction of his headquarters of Edo Castle. More than a hundred thousand men are put to work to dig wide moats, flatten hills, and heave into place the huge blocks of granite from which the walls and foundations are constructed. New western and northern wings are added, increasing the circumference of the main castle to a staggering ten miles.

Impressive though Edo Castle is, in the Kinai region the largest castle remains Ōsaka Castle, and it is there of all places that Toyotomi Hideyori is allowed to reside and receive vassals loyal to the Toyotomi cause. To dedicate himself to this problem, Ieyasu steps down as *shōgun* in favor of his son in 1605, only two years after he has assumed the title himself. Leaving Edo Castle to Hidetada, he moves to Sunpu Castle, from where he reinforces his clan's strategic position against the western warlords with renewed vigor, partly by consolidating his clan's ties with allies through intermarriage.

He has already tried this strategy on the Toyotomi in 1603, when he weds Hidetada's daughter, Sen-*hime*, off to Toyotomi Hideyori at the tender age of six. Yet despite an apparently happy marriage (the children play together happily), it does not produce the political stability Ieyasu envisioned. To his great chagrin, Hideyori remains under the influence of men with vehement anti-Tokugawa sentiments. Ieyasu's greatest antagonist at Ōsaka Castle, however, is a woman, Hideyori's mother Yodo-*dono*, who leaves no stone unturned to restore her crumbling family fortunes.

In 1611, in an effort to placate the House of Toyotomi, Ieyasu invites Hideyori to an audience at his Kyoto headquarters of Nijō Castle. Yodo-*dono* is fiercely opposed. but two influential *daimyō*, Katō Kiyomasa, and Asano Yoshinaga, manage to persuade Hideyori to make his appearance. Arriving at the castle's magnificent Kara Gate on the morning of 5 October, the nom-

Hideyori's audience with Ieyasu and his senior vassals

The Hōkō Temple bell and its offending characters (inset)

inal heir to Hideyoshi's realm emerges from his carriage to be met by a supplicant Ieyasu. The young man greets the *Tenka-dono* in the most polite manner, and for the next two hours the sixty-eight-year-old Ieyasu and the seventeen-year-old Hideyori exchange courtesies, drink cups of *sake*, and make each other gifts of exquisitely crafted swords.

It is not enough. Disgruntled chieftains and retainers keep coalescing around the young leader of the House of Toyotomi. For another three years, Ieyasu keeps his nerve. Then, in the summer of 1614, he finds the pretext he is looking for. It is while at Sunpu Castle, that he learns that the House of Toyotomi intends to celebrate the reconstruction of the Hōkō Temple in Kyoto with an inscription on the huge temple bell. Part of the long inscription contain the Chinese characters that make up the name Tokugawa, though they stand apart. Separating the two characters that make up his name, goes a step too far for the *Tenka-dono*: it suggests—so he says—the decapitation of the House of Tokugawa. He immediately orders all celebrations to be canceled, though he again carefully refrains from moving against Hideyori. Instead, he patiently waits for the Toyotomi camp to make the first move.

Toward the end of October, Ieyasu's spies inside Ōsaka Castle inform him that the Toyotomi are stocking up on rations and ammunition. They even have the temerity to raid his private *yashiki* within the castle compound—they are clearly preparing for a long, drawn-out siege. It will take a major effort to crush them; from his spies' detailed reports his advisors estimate that, backed by their allies, the Toyotomi will be able to muster as many as a hundred thousand warriors in all. Many of them are *rōnin*, *samurai* who have been left without a lord in the wake of Ieyasu's nationwide redistribution of territories. They are paid with the gigantic horde of gold bullion Hideyoshi had amassed during his lifetime and which now sits inside the *kinzō*, the two gold storages at the foot of the castle's magnificent 5-story keep.

Then, on 3 November word reaches Ieyasu that Hideyori has sent missives to befriended chieftains, calling on them to join him at Ōsaka Castle. Only few respond. One of them is Sanada Yukimura, who (encouraged by two hundred bars of gold sent by Hideyori) immediately declares himself for the Toyotomi.A few others, too, have joined the fray. Among them are Mōri Katsunaga, Chōsokabe Morichika, and Ban Naoyuki. They are, however, not major players. Others yet take a more ambivalent stance—Fukushima Masanori, for instance, who refuses to declare himself for Hideyori, though he does allow the latter's men to empty his storehouse within the castle grounds, which holds some eighty thousand *koku* worth of rice.

Thus it is that, with a handful of chieftains and some ninety thousand *rōnin*, Hideyori prepares for war. The castle they occupy is one of the most impressive strongholds in the country, with wide moats and huge walls crowned by multi-storied turrets, many of them newly built. Yet the castle has one major weak point. Sitting at the northern extremity of the Uemachi Plateau, it is well protected by the Yodo River from the north, but to the south, it lies exposed to the Ōsaka Hirano, a wide plain where huge armies can assemble to lay siege to the castle with impunity. And it is this Achilles heel that Ieyasu seeks to exploit when he decides to assemble his army south of the castle.

Sanada Yukimura (1567–1615), whose formal name was Sanada Nobushige, was born as the second son to Sanada Masayuki, the lord of Ueda Castle in northern Shinano Province and a vassal of the Takeda clan. Yukimura was only nine years old when, in 1575, two of his uncles died fighting for Takeda Katsuyori in the epic Battle of Nagashino, and his father became the head of the Sanada clan. After that, Yukimura spent much of his youth being sent from one castle to the other as a hostage in his father's attempts to keep his clan alive amid ever-shifting allegiances.

The real change in the fortunes of the young Yukimura and his clan came in 1585, when his father entered the service of Toyotomi Hideyoshi. Shortly afterward, Yukimura married the daughter of a Toyotomi vassal and, in 1590, had his first battle experience in the siege of Minowa Castle during Hideyoshi's vast campaign against the Hōjō at Odawara Castle. He and his father were mobilized, too, during Hideyoshi's invasion of the Korean Peninsula, though their contribution was limited to guarding his springboard of Nagoya Castle in Bizen, Kyūshū.

In the run-up to the Battle of Sekigahara Yukimura and his father declared themselves on the side of Ishida Mitsunari, even though his older brother, Nobuyuki, chose Ieyasu's side. They gave Hidetada a hard time when he diverted his forces from the Nakasendō to attack their stronghold of Ueda Castle. It did not go well for Hidetada, who failed to seize the castle and, as a result, failed to reach Sekigahara in time for the battle that mattered. Ieyasu must have been impressed with the Sanada warriors. After all, he too had tried and failed to reduce Ueda Castle several decades before. It was perhaps because of this—and because Nobuyuki had joined Ieyasu's side—that Yukimura and his father were spared Mitsunari's fate. Instead, they were exiled to Mount Kōya. There, both father and son languished in idleness until the summer of 1614, when on Hideyori's request, Yukimura rallied his Ueda retainers and joined those within Ōsaka Castle.

Ōsaka Castle in Hideyori's day

On November 11, Ieyasu departs from Sunpu at the head of a huge army. On its way southward along the Tōkaidō, it is joined by the forces of allied chieftains, so that by the time Ieyasu enters Nijō Castle in Kyoto, on 24 November, his army has swollen to a hundred thousand men. That same day, his son, *Shōgun* Hidetada, departs from Edo Castle at the head of another sixty thousand men. Despite the cold of winter and drifting snow, he and his men cover the three hundred miles in three weeks. By the time they arrive in Nara, on 15 December, his father has already set up his headquarters at Chausu-*yama*, a shallow hill some three miles south of Ōsaka Castle. The site Ieyasu has chosen is, in fact, hallowed ground: it is a former *kofun*, an imperial tomb that is already mentioned in the *Nihon shoki*.

Three days later, on 18 December, father and son have their first war council atop Chausu-*yama*. Hidetada proposes that they attack forthwith. Ieyasu dismisses the idea: though they might be in the majority, Ōsaka Castle is one of the most formidable castles in the realm—they would need double the men to reduce it that way. Instead, he decides on a strategy of encirclement. 'We must guard ourselves against the danger of making light of the enemy,' he admonishes his son, 'we must instead seek to conquer him without fighting him.' His son may be *shōgun*; it is Ieyasu who makes the decisions.

Inside the castle, meanwhile, the few chieftains who have rallied to Hideyori's cause are at loggerheads with his counselors. The latter favor a defensive approach. They feel that the castle with its deep moats and high walls is their best defense. Ieyasu's troops, they believe, will never be able to

Contemporary map of Chausu-*yama*

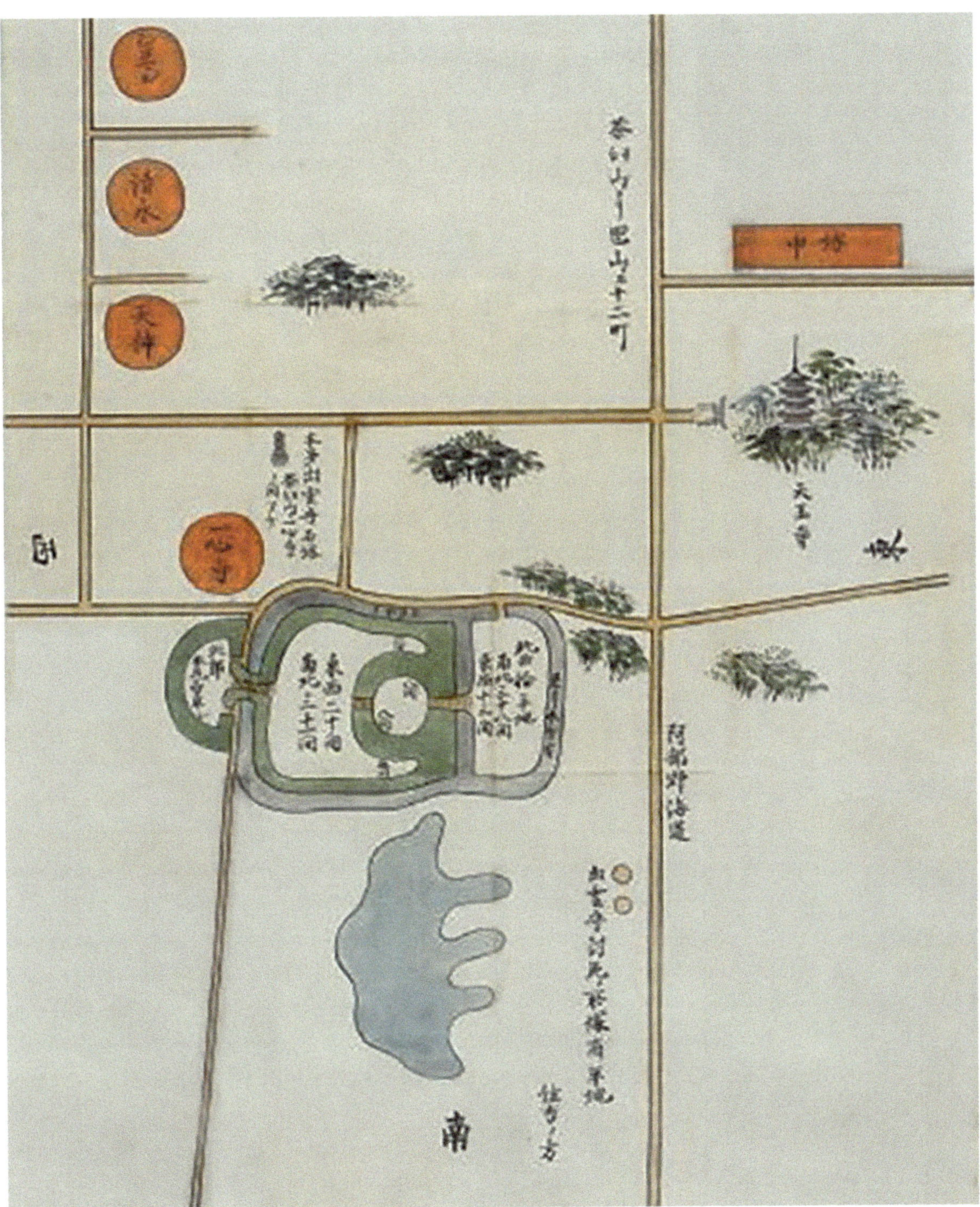
天王寺
南

take the fortress. It is also winter. Sooner or later cold and fatigue will get the better of the besieging troops and force Ieyasu to enter into negotiations—negotiations, so they believe, into which they will enter from a position of strength.

Their plan is heatedly contested by the chieftains. Most of them hate Ieyasu with a passion, a hatred only equaled by their respect for his military talent. The most forceful among them is Sanada Yukimura. He argues they ought to take the offensive and deal Ieyasu's army a decisive blow at the Seta River. The other chieftains agree. They know from experience that such a victory might persuade less bold chieftains to join their ranks. Only if they fail should they fall back on Ōsaka Castle. In the end, the counselors' strategy wins through, and one by one, albeit grudgingly, the chieftains fall into line, entrenching themselves as best they can among vast defenses in two extending circles around the stronghold.

Though Ieyasu has opted for a strategy of encirclement, it does not mean there is no fighting that winter. A cordon around such a vast castle—which has a circumference of ten miles—is not established overnight; there are numerous defensive positions around the castle that prevent his forces from doing so. These first have to be taken out. The first such engagement comes one day after Ieyasu and Hidetada's war council when, in the early dawn of 19 December, a contingent of some three thousand men led by Hachisuka Yoshishige, Asano Nagaakira (Nagamasa's son), and Ikeda Tadakatsu (Terumasa's son) attack a Toyotomi fort at the mouth of the Kizu River. Situated southwest of the castle, the fortification ensures a steady supply of provisions into the castle from Ōsaka Bay. It is being defended by some eight hundred warriors under the command of Akashi Teruzumi, a man who has proved his merit during the siege of Fushimi Castle and the Battle of Sekigahara under the command of Ukita Hideie. This is not true of Ieyasu's three commanders, especially Tadakatsu, who is still only twelve years old. Splitting into two groups, they launch a fierce attack on the fort over water with some forty vessels. The attack is a huge success, partly because, at that very moment, Teruzumi is at Ōsaka Castle for a war council.

The next clash comes a week later, this time on the opposite side of the castle, along the banks of the Yamato River. On the river's north bank, Ieyasu

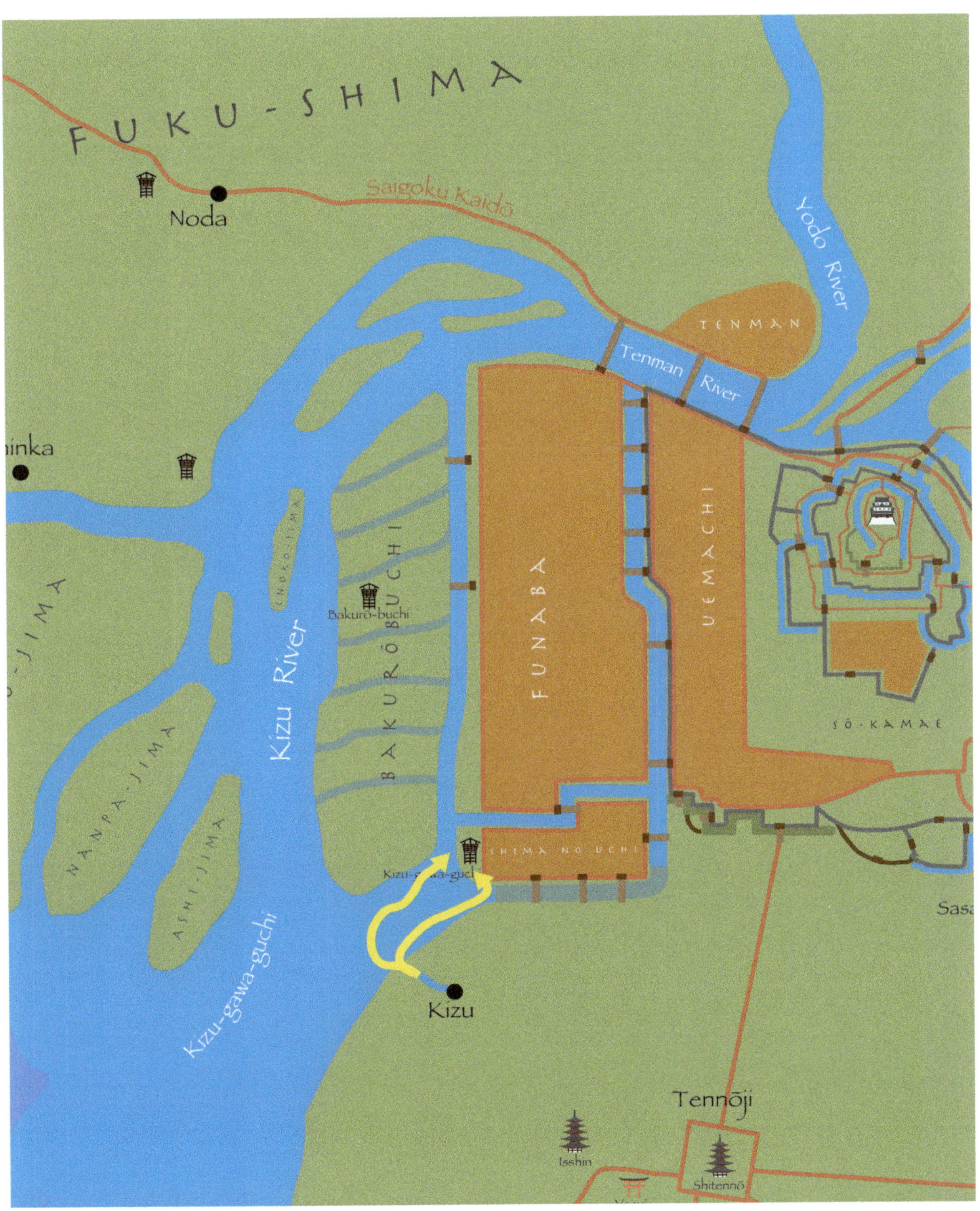
FUKU-SHIMA
Noda
Saigoku Kaidō
Yodo River
TENMAN
Tenman River
FUNABA
UEMACHI
SŌ·KAMAE
BAKURŌBUCHI
Bakurō-buchi
Kizu River
NANPA-JIMA
ASHI-JIMA
SHIMA NO UCHI
Kizu-gawa-guchi
Kizu
Tennōji
Isshin
Shitennō

intends to erect a *jinjō*, a makeshift fortress that will serve as a local headquarters for his troops on that side of the castle. Currently, the area is under the control of Toyotomi forces. At Shigino or 'Sandpiper Plain,' a flat piece of land wedged between the Hirano and Yamato rivers, they have erected a three-tier palisade that is defended by some two thousand men under the command of Inoue Yoritsugu. A smaller force of six hundred men under the command of Yano Masatomo and Iida Iesada have entrenched themselves in likewise fashion on the north bank of the river, near the hamlet of Imafuku. It is to dislodge them that Ieyasu gives two of his more seasoned commanders their brief. Uesugi Kagekatsu, who is encamped on the grounds of the Katsuragi Shrine, due east of the castle, is to attack the fortifications at Shigino. At the same time, Satake Yoshinobu is to attack the fortifications at Imafuku.

On 26 December, at the break of dawn, Kagekatsu leads some five thousand men northward and opens a withering attack against Sakai Yoritsugu's

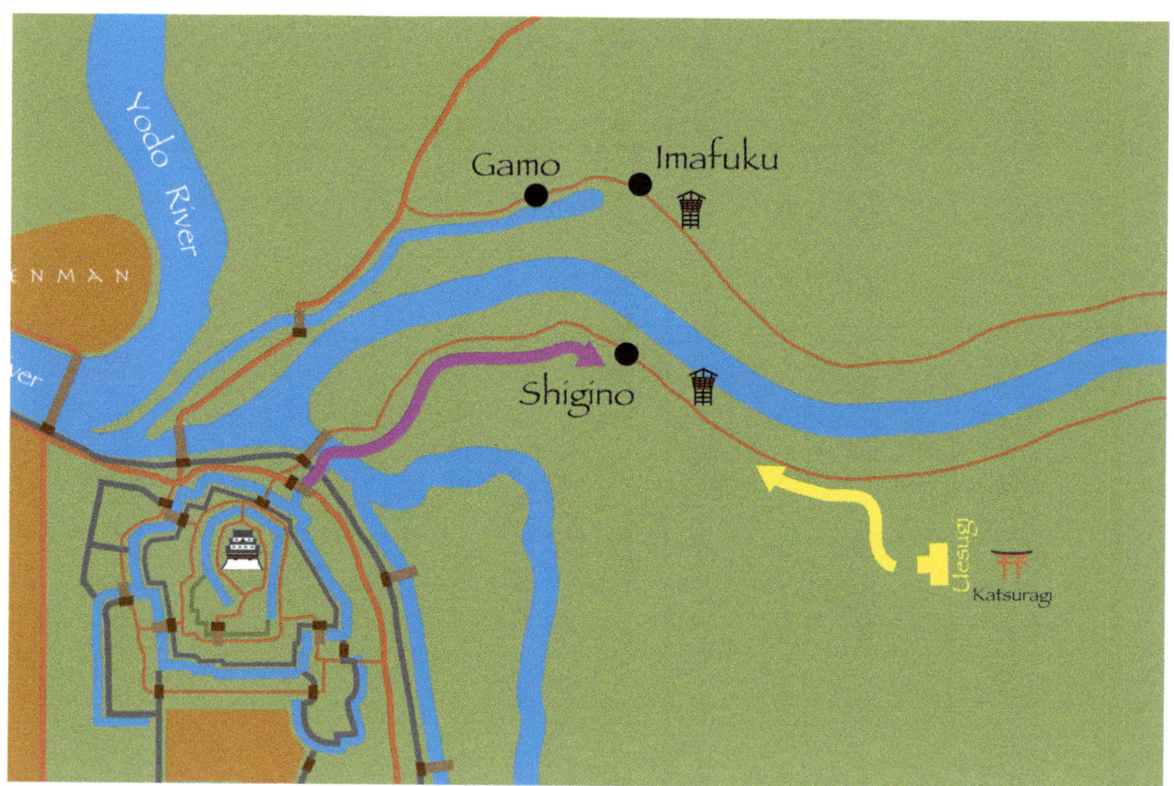

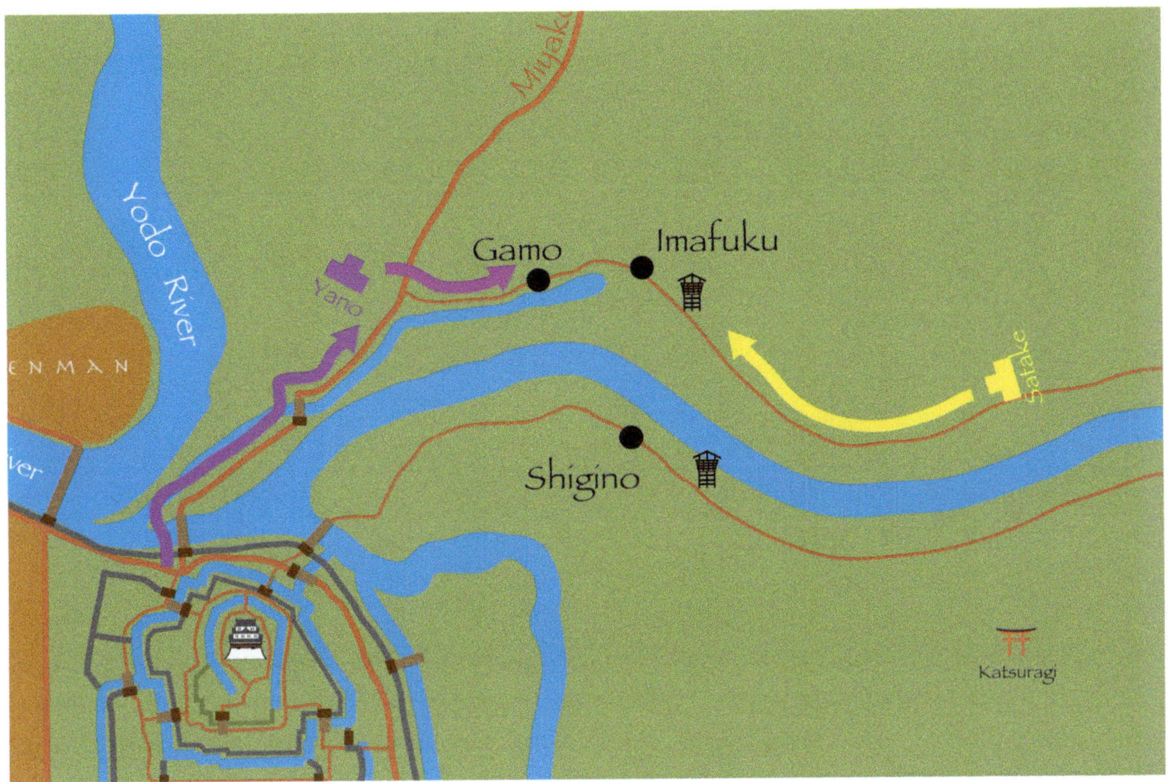

forces entrenched at Shigino. A fierce battle ensues in which Kagekatsu's men manage to penetrate as far as the inner palisade. Toward noon, Sakai Yoritsugu is killed in action, and for a moment it seems the fort is about to fall. But then a huge force of twelve thousand men under the command of Ōno Harunaga comes to their aid. They drive Kagekatsu's vanguard back toward the outer palisade, threatening to slaughter them when Suibara Chikanori, who commands a unit of Kagekatsu's *teppō ashigaru*, loudly orders them the stand aside. They do so, and in the next moment, a large number of Harunaga's men are wiped out by a hail of bullets.

Meanwhile, on the river's opposite bank, Satake Yoshinobu, who has only fifteen hundred men at his disposal, runs into similar trouble. He and his men also manage to reach the fortification's inner defenses. But then they come under fire from a unit of *teppō ashigaru* under the command of Kimura Shigenari and suffer a great number of casualties. By noon the fighting has

Kimura Shigenari at Imafuku

reached a deadlock, with Yoshinobu's men maintaining a precarious stand. Observing the fighting from the main keep of his castle, Hideyori sends Gotō Mototsugu with three thousand men toward Imafuku to swing the balance in their favor. With his help, the defenders manage to drive the attackers back toward the fortification's outer defenses and kill one of Yoshinobu's commanders.

It is amidst this general standoff on both sides of the river that reinforcements under the command of Horio Tadaharu, Niwa Nagashige, and Sakakibara Yasukatsu come to the rescue of the attackers and that, toward the end of the day and many casualties amidst yet more hard fighting, the two fortifications are finally captured.

Two more obstacles thwart Ieyasu's goal to encircle the castle. One is located west of the castle, at the center of Bakurōbuchi, an outlying piece of flatland bordering the Kizu River, where some seven hundred Toyotomi forces man another makeshift fortification. The other is at Noda, at the center of Fukushima, one of the larger islands at the mouth of the Yodo River. At Shinka, on the southside of the island, the Toyotomi forces have their *funakura*, the boathouses for their defensive fleet. The area is heavily fortified, much of it using remnants of the former Ishiyama Hongan-*ji*, the temple complex that held out so long under Oda Nobunaga's siege. They are guarded by some eight hundred men under the command of Ōno Harutane.

On 28 December, in the dead of night, while the region is lashed by a torrential downpour, a force of six thousand Tokugawa warriors embark from Denpō-*guchi* at the mouth of the Yodo River in a fleet of a hundred and fifty vessels. Navigating the treacherous channels among the vast cluster of islands and sandbanks at the mouth of the river, they make their way to the southern tip of Fukushima and launch a surprise attack on the stationed Toyotomi troops. The latter are utterly taken by surprise and Harutane and his men almost immediately desert their positions to flee toward Tenman, on the east side of the island, and from there toward the castle.

By dawn, a second assault is underway, this one against the makeshift fortification at Bakurōbuchi. It is equally successful, not because its defenders don't put up a fight, but because its commander, Susukida Kanesuke, is absent. He is not even at Ōsaka Castle, but over at Kanzaki, a red light district

FUKU-SHIMA
Noda
Saigoku Kaidō
Yodo River
TENMAN
Tenman
River
FUNABA
UEMACHI
SŌ-KAMAE
Kizu River
Bakurōbuchi
BAKURŌBUCHI
NANPA-JIMA
ASHI-JIMA
SHIMA NO UCHI
Kizu-gawa-guchi
Kizu-gawa-guchi
Asano
Kizu
Tennōji
Isshin
Shitennō

on the north bank of the Yodo River. As at Noda, the attack is a resounding success. Kanesuke's absence and Ōno Harutane's cowardice in the face of danger earn the two men the eternal scorn of their fellow warriors and Ōsaka's populace. They are laughingly referred to as a *daidai-musha* or '*daidai* warriors,' the *daidai* being a bitter orange whose only use is for New Year's decorations.

With the fall of the last two fortifications, the *soto-kamae* or 'outer defense,' is broken, and the ring around the castle is closed; those inside the castle are now hermetically sealed off from the outside world and, with it, any hope of assistance. Having distributed his forces in a wide circle around the castle, Ieyasu—for it is he still who makes the calls—can now turn his attention to the castle itself.

Though the Toyotomi forces have now lost all their outlying fortifications, they can still rely on Ōsaka Castle's formidable defenses. Some of those defenses are natural: the wide Kizu River toward the west, the Tenma River toward the north, and the Nekoma and Hirano rivers toward the east. The castle's heavily fortified inner citadel is furthermore surrounded by two wide baileys, each surrounded by high walls and deep moats. The stronghold, however, has one Achilles heel: the vast plain that lies south of the castle, and it is exactly there where Ieyasu has amassed the bulk of his force. It is to counter this weak point that, in the run-up to the siege, Sanada Yukimura has erected the Sanada-*maru*, an outer bailey that sits along the ridge of one of the few elevations in the flat landscape, just outside the castle's southern wall where it is not protected by a moat. The Sanada-*maru* is a fort in its own right. It is surrounded by a high earthen rampart crowned with a raised parapet from behind which *teppō ashigaru* can fire on the enemy without being exposed. It also serves as a major *umadashi*, a 'horse breakout' from which sorties can be launched.

Positioned immediately south of the Sanada-*maru* are the twelve thousand men of Maeda Toshitsune, the son of the great Maeda Toshiie and the husband of Hidetada's daughter Tama-*hime*. He has been ordered by Ieyasu to dig trenches and raise ramparts opposite the barbican, but not to attack it. Toshitsune dutifully complies and sets his men to work during the first days of January. No sooner have they started, however, than they come under fire

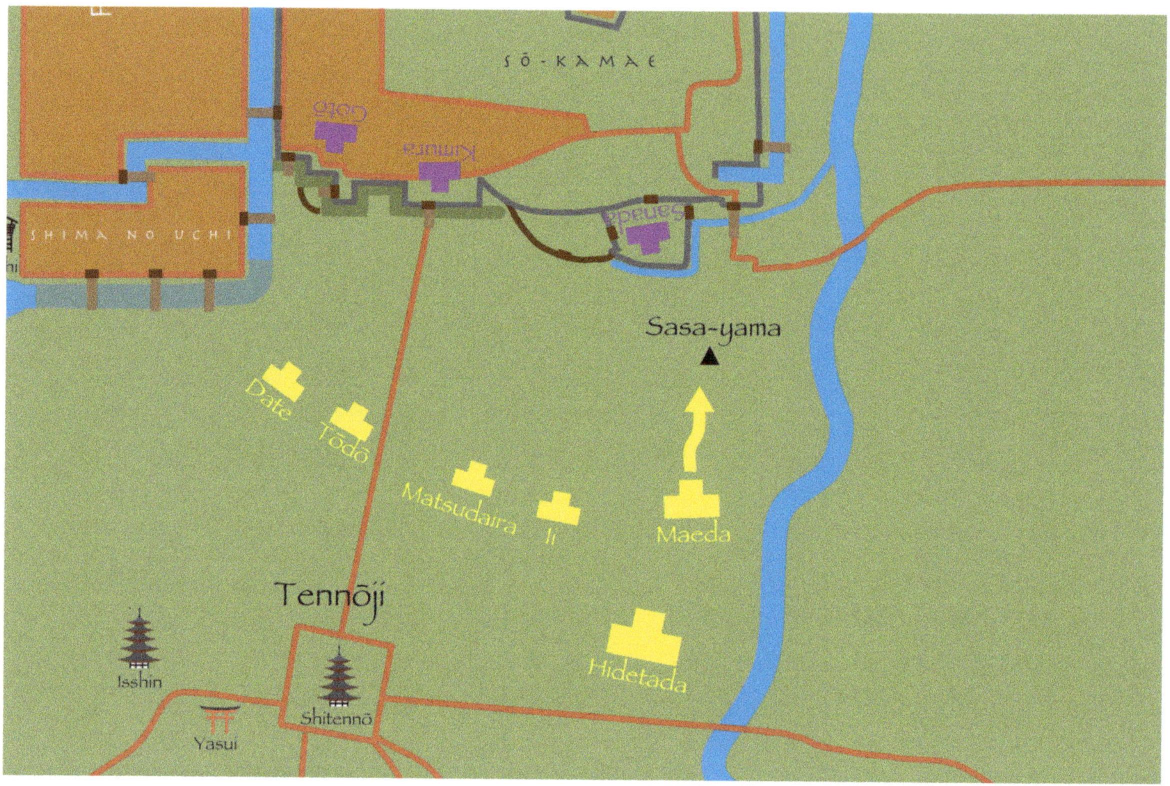

from Yukimura's *teppō ashigaru*, who have taken up position on Sasa-*yama*, a shallow hill at a stone's throw south of the Sanada-*maru*. To rid himself of this nuisance, Toshitsune and his commanders devise a plan to drive the enemy back toward the Sanada-*maru*, albeit without informing either Hidetada or Ieyasu of their plans.

On January 3, in the dead cold of night, two of Toshitsune's commanders—Honda Masashige and Yamazaki Naganori—lead an elite spearhead in a surprise attack against the *teppō ashigaru* positioned atop the hill. To their surprise, however, they find no one there. Shortly before the Tokugawa attack, Yukimura's *teppō ashigaru* have abandoned their positions atop the hill and have withdrawn to the safety of the barbican, from where they again pick off Toshitsune's men with impunity. It leads Toshitsune and his commanders to suspect that somebody within the castle is being fed information about their movements.

The next day, disappointment among Toshitsune's spearhead makes way for enraged indignation when Yukimura's *teppō ashigaru* within the Sanada-*maru*, who are now well within earshot, begin to taunt them from the safety of their defenses. By noon the tale of their futile venture has been cast in song, yelled down at them gleefully from above with ever-increasing mirth. Cold and riled by their detractors, the men among the spearhead can contain themselves no longer and begin to attack the barbican itself, only to come under yet more fire from atop, causing a great number of casualties among the hapless men, who, for inexplicable reasons, have not brought along their iron-clad shields and are now forced to slowly struggle toward the top behind sandbags they have to push uphill in front of them.

The fierce contest for the Sanada-*maru*

Just then, the castle's powder magazine detonates. Spotting the huge billowing cloud that rises above the castle keep, the besieging forces take it as a sign from their informant, Nanjō Mototada, within the castle. Two young and impressionable commanders, Ii Naotaka and Matsudaira Tadanao, take the sign to mean that Mototada's forces guarding the Hirano-bashi are about to attack those within the Sanada-*maru* from behind. In truth, no such thing is happening: Mototada has been exposed and killed and his men remain in place. As a result, their frontal assault on the barbican strikes its defenses like a wave does a rock: it exhausts itself and recedes without effect, leaving in its wake a field strewn with the bodies of dead and wounded warriors.

That evening, Ieyasu summons all the commanders involved in the debacle to his headquarters atop Chausu-*yama*. There, in the presence of his son and his other senior generals, he openly scolds them for embarking on such a Quixotic and doomed mission. He makes a point of putting Maeda Toshitsune in his place—he might be married to Ieyasu's granddaughter, but that does not mean he can disregard his strict orders. Most outraged of all he is with Toshitsune for sending his men into combat without their shields. If he should ever have the audacity to launch a similar escapade again, he should at least have the decency to provide his men with sufficient protection!

Ieyasu's headquarters at Chausu-*yama* (right)

Cannon begin to pound the castle's defenses

Meanwhile, inside the citadel, the Toyotomi commanders congratulate Sanada Yukimura on his brilliant route. Some make the most of what they assume will be their imminent moment of glory. Oda Yorigana, a cousin of the great Nobunaga, makes the rounds of the guards on horseback. Unlike his great rival Ieyasu, who likes to dress plainly, he is clad in gilt-laced armor with autumn-tinted thread. His attendant is a young woman warrior, in scarlet armor, with scarlet scabbards, and a scarlet arrow catcher gracing her slender back.

The festive mood inside the castle does not last. During the second week of January, Ieyasu's troops begin to pound the stronghold from the south with cannon, most of them from the Kunitomo foundry in Nagahama, on the eastern shore of Lake Biwa, and the Shibatsuji foundry in Negoro. On Bizen-*jima*, a small island in a curve of the Yodo River, a hundred gunners take aim at the stronghold using so-called *ōzuchu*, handheld and ground-placed mortars that

The indomitable Yodo-*dono*

can hurl rounds of up to a pound over a distance of up to a mile. To enhance their effect, Ieyasu orders all the two-hundred thousand assembled troops to raise the battle cry and to fire their muskets every day for the remainder of the siege. They are to do so at three designated times: late in the afternoon, the hour of the Rooster; late in the evening, the hour of the Dog; and in the dead of night, the hour of the Tiger. The effect is mind-shattering, robbing the castle's defenders of their nightly rest. The collective report of their arms and their united roar is so loud that it can be heard as far away as Kyoto, some thirty miles away.

To drive his message further home, Ieyasu orders his archers to hurl arrows into the enemy camp carrying leaflets in which they are urged to surrender. One person, however, remains undaunted, the indomitable Yodo-*dono*. She refuses to even consider surrender, urging her son to turn down the enemy's attempts at a negotiated settlement. Hoisting herself and four of her consorts into full armor, she goes out onto the castle's ramparts to spur on the troops who man the barricades.

But even the headstrong Yodo-*dono* cannot negate the devastating effect the enemy's heavy cannon are having on those around her. Positioned on Bizen-*jima* and at Tennōji-*guchi* (just east of Chausu-*yama*), they are well within range of the stronghold's inner citadel. Their range at Bizen-*jima* allows the gunners to aim for the castle's main keep, which is situated at the northeast corner of the inner citadel. Many of the projectiles from Tennōji-*guchi*, however, fall short of their target, landing instead on the two sprawling residential quarters of Hideyori and his entourage. On the first day, a thirteen-pound cannonball crashes through the roof of the Oku-*goten*, Hideyori's private quarters at the foot of the keep, where the womenfolk resided, instantly killing two of Yodo-*dono*'s maidens. More strikes follow so that, within the space of just a few days, she loses eight of her maids, most of them after an agonizing struggle with death. It is their loss, more than all the men that have perished over the previous weeks, that breaks her spirit. Deeply shaken by the death of her maidens, Yodo-*dono* relents and tells her son to seek an end to the torment.

After a short war council at his severely damaged Omote-*goten* at the inner citadel's south side, Hideyori and his elders decide to appoint the monk

and tea master Oda Nagamasu (the younger brother of Oda Nobunaga) as their envoy. He is to try and negotiate a truce. On 11 January, he and Ōno Harunaga hold lengthy talks with Honda Masazumi, Ieyasu's chief of staff and one of the *bakufu*'s Council of Elders. The talks end in failure.

In truth, though he has the upper hand in sheer numbers, Ieyasu, too, is keen to reach a settlement. For one, he riles at the thought of seeing Hideyori perish—the boy remains, after all, the son of Hideyoshi, a man to whom Ieyasu has solemnly sworn his allegiance. Winter is by now also setting in hard, and though his generals have made great efforts to acquire sufficient provisions, feeding two hundred thousand men who are fighting off the biting cold is a huge logistical challenge, especially since the Toyotomi camp has bought up all the local cereals in the run-up to the siege. If those inside the castle play their hand well, that siege could take many more months. Ending the siege at this stage with a negotiated settlement will solve all his problems.

Not that Ieyasu lets his eagerness show. He flatly turns down the first offer from the Toyotomi camp: to send Yodo-*dono* as a hostage to Edo on the condition that all *rōnin* inside the castle be restored to their former lands—this is simply inconceivable. A second offer, this time through the mediation of none other than the Imperial Court in Kyoto, is equally rebuffed. If there are to be any negotiations, they are to be conducted on the initiative and in the camp of the Tokugawa. Those conditions are met on 17 January, when Yodo-*dono*'s younger sister, the shrewd Jōkō'in, visits the camp of Kyōgoku Tadataka, a man who had fought alongside Ishida Mitsunari in the Battle of Sekigahara but who has since gone over to Ieyasu's side.

Negotiations get off to a good start. Katagiri Katsumoto, who is in command of a group of artillerymen stationed at Bizen-*jima*, gets wind of their progress. He has a keen interest in their outcome. It had been Katsumoto, after all, who, four months earlier, had been commissioned with the founding of the temple bell for the Hōkō Temple, and it was Katsumoto who had selected the controversial inscription. He had even gone up to Sunpu to explain matters, but Ieyasu had refused to even see him. His efforts had been poorly rewarded. On his return to Ōsaka—for he was then still a Toyotomi elder—he had been put under house arrest at his *yashiki* within the castle's second

Katagiri Katsumoto (1556–1615) was a native of Ōmi Province and born into a clan of warriors in the service of Azai Nagamasa, the lord of Odani Castle. He was only fourteen years old when, in 1570, Oda Nobunaga laid siege to Odani Castle and when Nagamasa, just before he was about to commit *seppuku*, sent Katsumoto's father a letter to thank him for his steadfast service.

When Toyotomi Hideyoshi occupied the former Azai stronghold of Nagahama Castle in 1573 and hired local warriors to man it, Katsumoto seized the chance and entered Hideyoshi's service. Katsumoto proved a loyal and capable retainer. Over the next decades, he participated in most of Hideyoshi's battles. He was there at the Battle of Shizugatake as one of the Seven Spearmen of Shizugatake, Hideyoshi's mounted bodyguard. The next year, he took part in the battles of Komaki and Nagakute, when he commanded a mounted guard of 150 men. He took part in Hideyoshi's campaigns in Chūgoku and Kyūshū, as well as his disastrous invasion of the Korean Peninsula.

Katsumoto's talents were not just limited to the martial; his civic contributions were equally impressive. Already during the late 1580s, he was in charge of roadworks as *dōsaku bugyō* to ease the logistics during Hideyoshi's campaign in western Japan. In its wake, he held the position of *kenchi bugyō*, overseeing the extensive land surveys necessary for the redistribution of lands. The next decade found him at Fushimi, where he was part of the team of magistrates (*fushin bugyō*) in charge of the construction of Fushimi Castle.

It was in a civil capacity, too, that Katsumoto decided to support Ishida Mitsunari in the run-up and during the Battle of Sekigahara. For this, he was pardoned, and after 1603, he accepted the authority of the *bakufu*. He remained a retainer of the Toyotomi, however, and climbed to the rank of senior elder to Hideyoshi's son, Hideyori.

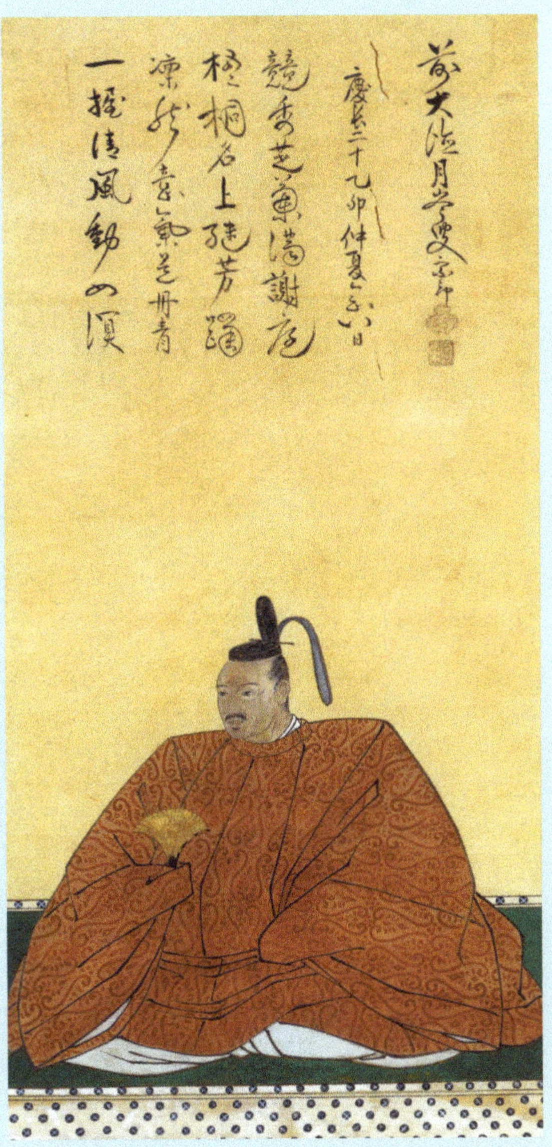

bailey on suspicions of being in cahoots with the *bakufu*. There, he was being harassed continually by retainers from the likes of Ōno Harunaga. When word reached Katsutomo that Harunaga planned to assassinate him, he told his men to arm themselves. For Hideyori and his mother, who had up till then kept their faith in their elder, it was a step too far, and they had ordered him to leave the castle grounds. In the early morning of 3 November, Katsumoto left Ōsaka and had withdrawn to his military headquarters of Ibaraki Castle in northern Settsu. It was that same day, that Ieyasu heard of Katsumoto's eviction and Hideyori's mobilization, and that he had decided to lay siege to the castle. Three weeks later, Katsumoto was present when, on 24 November, Ieyasu arrived at Nijō Castle to hold his first war council.

Given all his efforts for a peaceful settlement, the fifty-eight-year-old Katsumoto is delighted with the news. He is so excited, indeed, that he cannot keep from writing to his good friend, the abbot Junnyo of the Nishi Hongan-*ji*, a Buddhist temple of the Jōdo Shinshū in Kyoto:

> To the Abbot Junnyo,
>
> Thank you for kindly sending over your messenger and especially for the splendid parcels of delicacies.
>
> I am currently stationed at Bizen-*jima*, and the *Shōgun*, who honored us with a visit to inspect the troops this morning, was in very high spirits. It seems that those from the castle have come over to offer various apologies, and he expects a peace settlement within the next few days.
>
> This is joyous news indeed!
>
> I will let you know as soon as I hear what the results are.
>
> Katagiri Katsumoto

Hideyori has good reasons to be optimistic; by the end of the next day, the negotiators have hammered out the conditions under which peace can be restored. Those conditions are simple: the castle's second and third baileys—including all their defensive structures and moats—are to be dismantled;

only the inner citadel and its moat are to remain. In return, Hideyori can hang on to his territories and the assembled *rōnin* will be pardoned. Yodo-*dono* also does not have to travel up to Edo; instead, Ōno Harunaga and Oda Nagamasu are to provide hostages. On 19 January, in the nineteenth year of Keichō (1615), the signed pledges having been exchanged, the guns fall silent.

Work on the dismantlement of the castle's second and third bailey starts within days of the peace settlement. It has been agreed that both parties are to participate in dismantlement: the second bailey and inner moat are to be demolished and filled in by the House of Toyotomi; the third bailey and the outer moat by the House of Tokugawa. Eager to return home, Ieyasu places the latter project under the supervision of his son. Though it sounds like a vast undertaking, it should not take him long. Under the existing conventions, the dismantlement of baileys is a largely symbolic gesture, in which the victorious parties usually limited themselves to only tearing some of the structures down and filling in part of the moats. As usual, Hidetada sees things differently from his father; as the new *shōgun*, he is intent on interpreting the treaty to the letter. He appoints three chieftains (Honda Tadamasa, Honda Yasunori, and Matsudaira Tadaaki) as *umetate bugyō*, his 'deconstruction magistrates.' Three other commanders (Honda Masazumi, Andō Naotsugu, and Naruse Masanari) are appointed to provide the men and to press-gang the local populace into a vast workforce to carry out the massive project.

Spurred on relentlessly by Hidetada's construction magistrates, the work proceeds at such a pace that, despite the freezing cold, the southern section of the outer moat is filled in by the beginning of February. Still not satisfied, Hidetada orders his magistrates to 'assist' the Toyotomi camp with filling in the moat surrounding the castle's second bailey—work on which has proceeded at a far slower pace. All the defensive structures are torn down to the last beam and stone. Those *buke yashiki* that stand in the way are summarily torn down, without even consulting their owners. In his own mind, Hidetada has reason to be pleased with himself; by the time he sets off for Edo, on February 16, the southern crescents of the outer two moats, from the eastern Tamazukuri-*guchi* to the southwestern Ikutama-*guchi*, have been completely filled in. The Sanada-*maru*, too, has been dismantled.

Not surprisingly, the Toyotomi camp is less pleased with Hidetada's 'help;' there is much discontent among their warriors about the break with convention, especially among the retainers who have lost their *yashiki*. Disgruntled *rōnin* begin to run amok, first at Ōsaka, where they begin to dig out sections of moats that have just been filled in by Hidetada's workforce. On 12 April, no longer able to contain their hatred of the Tokugawa, they swarm out toward Fushimi and Kyoto, where they set fire to the *yashiki* of *bakufu* officials. Informed of the violence by his deputy in Kyoto, Itakura Katsushige, Ieyasu, who has meanwhile arrived back in Sunpu, demands that the offending *rōnin* be expelled from Ōsaka Castle. Hideyori does no such thing. Instead, he rewards them with new payments from the castle's two gold storages and tells them to get ready for another siege. That siege, Hideyori and his councilors realize, can no longer be won by entrenching themselves in their stronghold. Two of the castle's moats have been filled in on the side where the castle is most vulnerable: toward the south, especially without the Sanada-*maru*. Worse still, not all of the *rōnin* who have stood with them through the Winter Siege are still with them; many—some twenty thousand—have left the castle. As a result, there are now only some seventy thousand warriors left. It is clear that this time around they have to fight an offensive battle, meeting the enemy out in the field to try and deal them a decisive blow before they can reach the castle.

Ieyasu, meanwhile, because of the short notice, is also struggling to raise troops. To make up for the lacking numbers, he is forced to call on Kuroda Nagamasa, who had been guarding Edo Castle during the winter campaign. Even Katō Yoshiaki, who had been forced to remain behind in Edo because of his clan's strong ties with the House of Toyotomi, is ordered to mobilize his men. When, on 19 May 1615, Ieyasu and Hidetada rendezvous at Nijō Castle for a war council with their generals—Tōdō Takatora, Honda Masazumi, and Doi Toshikatsu—it is clear they have almost fifty thousand men less at their disposal than only three months earlier. Still, at more than one hundred and fifty thousand, it is double the number they are being fed by their informants at Ōsaka.

Ieyasu decides to split his army into two forces. One is to proceed along the Kyō Kaidō, which follows the south bank of the Yodo River toward

Ōsaka; the other is to take the Nara Kaidō toward Nara and then move west toward Dōmyōji following the same road along the south bank of the Yamato River. In addition, Asano Nagaakira, the lord of Wakayama Castle in Ise, is to lead his troops northward along the Kishū Kaidō toward Sakai.

Events almost overtake Ieyasu and his seasoned generals. On 23 May, seeking to achieve the coveted preemptive blow, Ōno Harufusa departs from

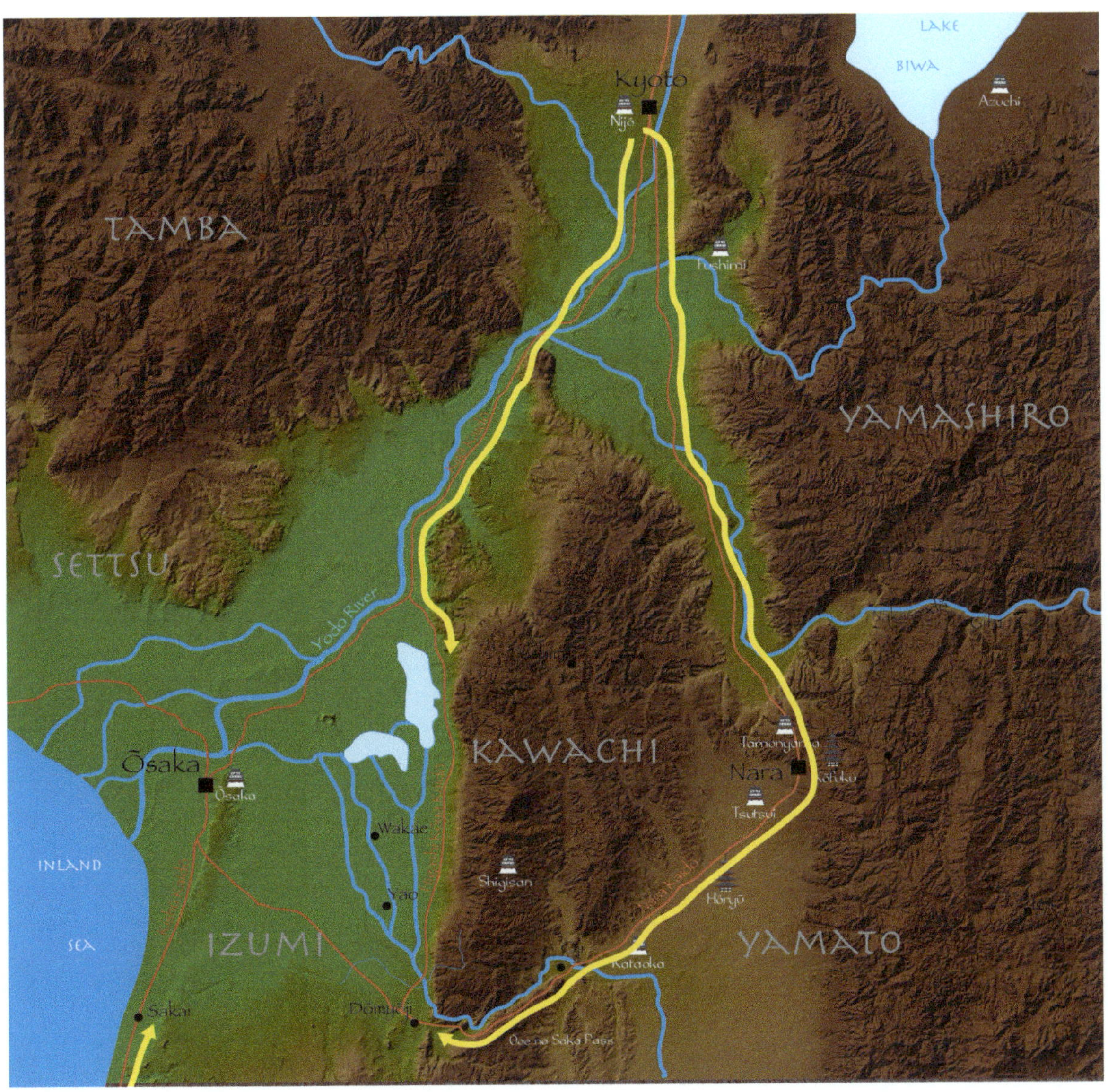

Ōsaka Castle at the head of a force of three thousand men. Marching eastward, they cross the Kuragari Pass and attack Kōriyama Castle, just west of Nara. It is the stronghold of Tsutsui Jōkei, who, in spite of repeated requests, has refused to join the Toyotomi side. Jōkei, who unlike his illustrious adoptive father, Junkei, has no battle experience whatsoever, abandons his castle and flees east into the Yoshino Mountains. His brother, Yoshiyuki, does put up a fight, but most of the retainers have fled in Jōkei's wake and he is forced to the Kōfuku Temple. From there, he organizes the defense of Nara's western

Contemporary map of Kōriyama Castle and its castle town

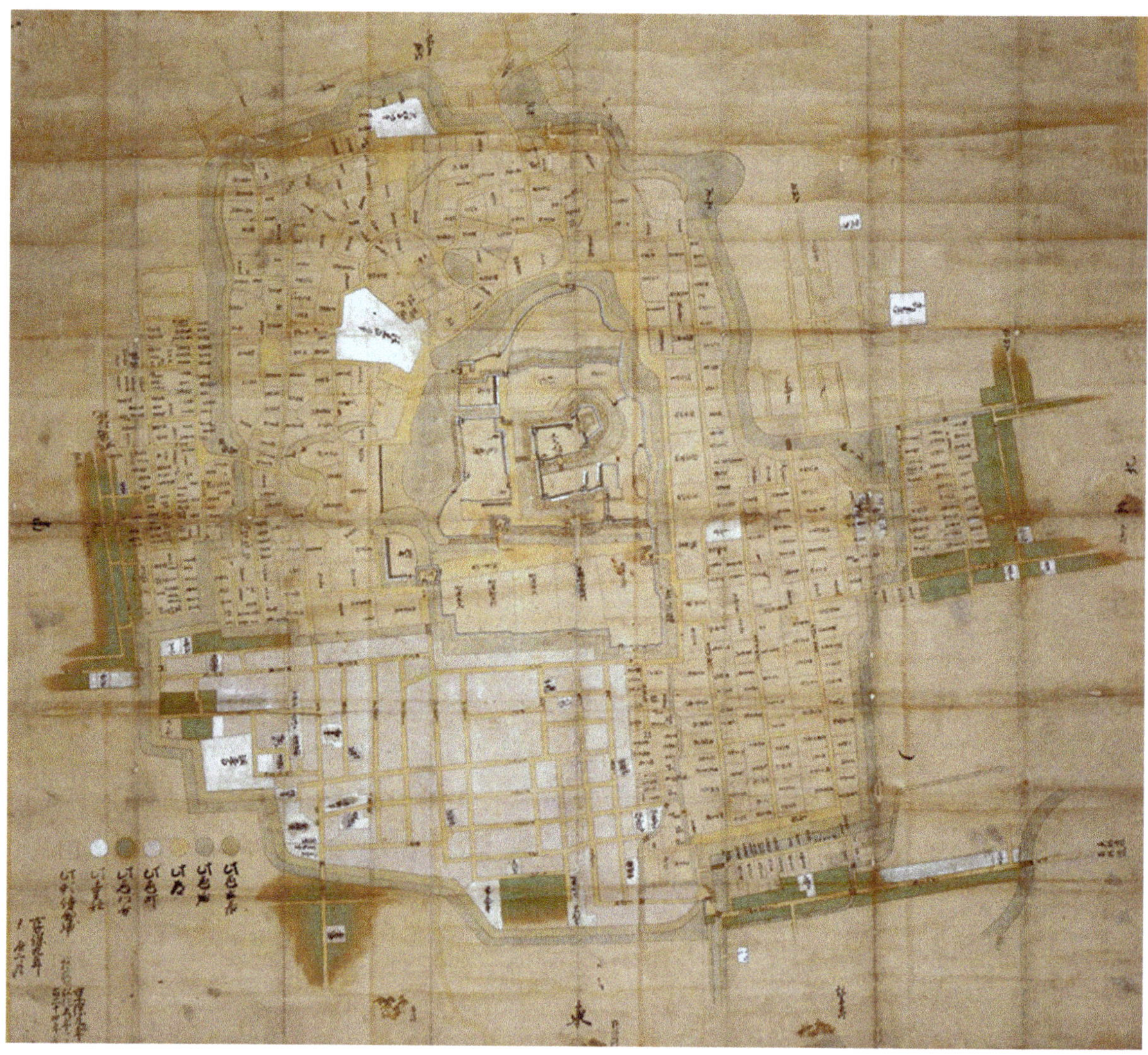

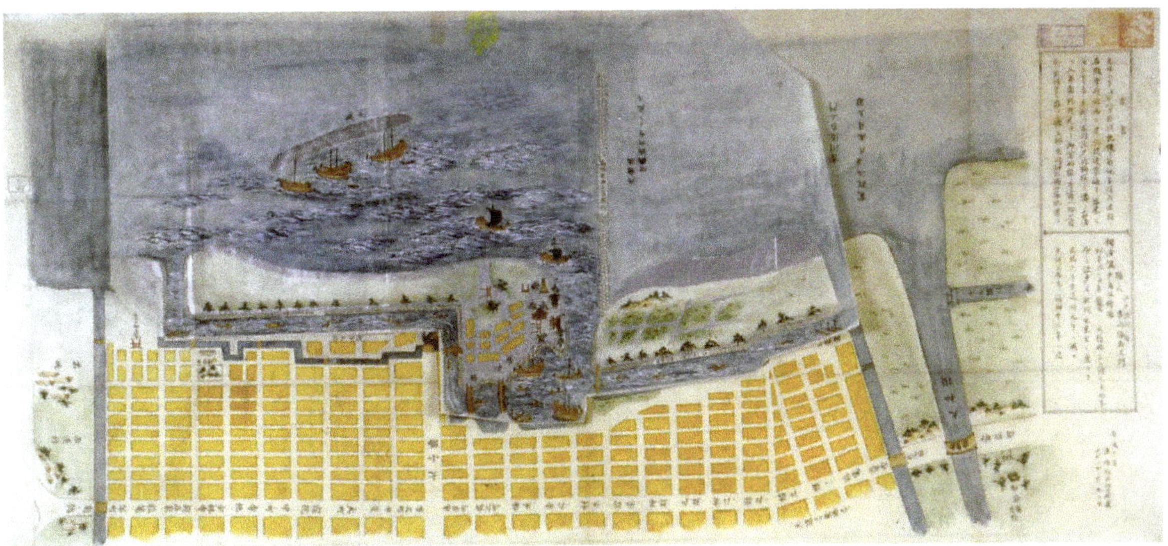

The port of Sakai

approaches. It saves the temple town from Harufusa's men, but not Kōriyama Castle, which along with most of its castle town goes up in flames.

Next, Harufusa's younger brother, Harutane, marches on Ieyasu's supply base of Sakai, indiscriminately setting fire to villages and farms along the way. Much of Sakai, too, is sacked. But when, on 26 May, Harufusa marches toward Wakayama Castle, he is intercepted halfway there by its lord Asano Nagaakira, who, in response to Ieyasu's request, has raised some five thousand men. What follows is a fierce clash on the banks of the Kashii River in which two of Harufusa's fellow commanders (Ban Naoyuki and Tannowa Shigemasa) lose their lives and one (Okabe Noritsuna) flees the field of battle. For another week, Harufusa and his men hold the line but when, on 2 June, he learns that Ieyasu's troops are approaching, he orders the remainder of his men to fall back toward the castle.

The Toyotomi, however, have not given up on their strategy to strike first. In the dead of night of that same day, 2 June, Gotō Mototsugu and three thousand men depart from Ōsaka Castle and head down the Nara Kaidō. It is the spearhead of a force of some twenty thousand men who are to intercept the eastern prong of the Tokugawa forces who are moving west along the high road. During a war council, while encamped at Tennōji the previous day, Mototsugu, Sanada Yukimura, and Mōri Katsunaga have de-

Gotō Mototsugu and his men reach the west bank of the Ishi River

cided to ambush the enemy at the village of Dōmyōji. Just east of the village, the mountains form a kettle where they can trap the enemy before the high road enters the wide plain south of the castle.

Mototsugu and his spearhead reach Dōmyōji well before dawn. Dense fog envelops the village, which sits on the west bank of the Ishi River, a side stream that joins the Yamato River just north of the village. Mototsugu is worried. The plan was to converge the rest of their forces at the village, but there is no sign of the rest of his own main force of six thousand men, nor is there any news from Yukimura's and Katsunaga's rear guard of twelve thousand. Worse still, his scouts who have gone ahead, inform him that the enemy, a spearhead under the banner of Mizuno Katsunari, have already set up camp at Kokubu, a hamlet just east of the Ishi River. Between Kokubu and the river sits a small hill by the name of Komatsu-*yama*. Unwilling to wait for reinforcements, Mototsugu decides to put the terrain to his advantage and orders his men to ford the river and take up positions atop the hill.

By the time Mototsugu and his men reach the top of the shallow hill at four in the morning, they run into two enemy units under the command of Matsukura Shigemasa and Okuda Tadatsugu. In this first clash, Tadatsugu loses his life, and Shigemasa is forced to withdraw. But then Mizuno Katsunari

Gotō Mototsugu (1560–1615) was born as the second son of Gotō Motokuni, a retainer to the Bessho clan of Harima Province. It was probably somewhere in the late seventies, when Mototsugu (who was then still called Matabei) entered the service of Sengoku Hidehisa, a vassal of Toyotomi Hideyoshi who went on the become the lord of Sumoto Castle on Awaji Island. As such, Mototsugu fought in Hideyoshi's campaign to subdue the island of Kyūshū. But when, during that campaign, Hidehisa suffered a crushing defeat in the Battle of Hetsugu-*gawa*, Mototsugu left his service and became a *yoriki* (police officer) on a stipend of 100 koku in the ranks of Kuriyama Toshiyasu, a senior vassal to Kuroda Yoshitaka.

It was in the service of the Kuroda that Mototsugu took part in numerous battles and sieges in Kyūshū and that, during the nineties, he crossed over to the Korean Peninsula during Hideyoshi's two campaigns to subdue its kingdoms. On the peninsula, he fought under the command of Katō Kiyomasa in the celebrated two sieges of Jinju Fort, where he is said to have been among the first to breach its defenses in the second siege.

During the Battle of Sekigahara, Mototsugu fought under Yoshitaka's son, Nagamasa, when he took the head of Ōhashi Kamon, a retainer of Ishida Mitsunari. It was on the strength of his performance in that battle that he was raised to the position of senior vassal and made the lord of Masutomi Castle and its domain of 10.000 koku. Yet his relationship with the young Nagamasa was never cordial and when, in 1604, Yoshitaka passed away, Mototsugu and his family left his service and abandoned their castle.

Mototsugu next entered the service of Hosokawa Tadaoki. But soon his relations with Tadaoki, too, soured and it was only through Ieyasu's intervention that he was able to extricate himself from his ties to the Hosokawa. In 1611, Kuroda Nagamasa made several attempts to again recruit Mototsugu but failed. And when, in the summer of 1614, □no Harunaga approached him to join him at Ōsaka Castle, Mototsugu threw in his lot with the Toyotomi.

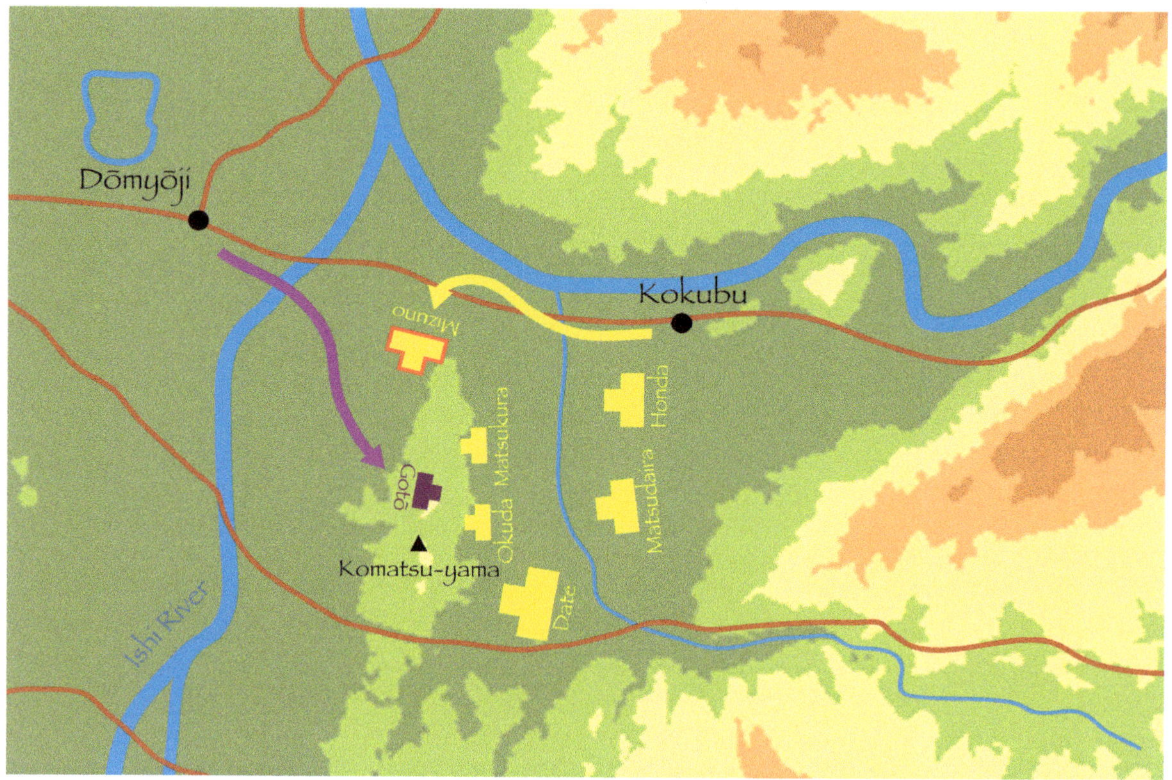

executes a brilliant pincer movement, trapping Mototsugu and his men atop the hill, where they come under fire from a unit of *teppō ashigaru* under the command of Katakura Shigenaga. One bullet hits Mototsugu, who orders his men to retreat back across the river toward Dōmyōji. Being surrounded, they have to fight their way back. By noon, after almost eight hours of heavy fighting, some make it back across the river. Mototsugu is not among them. Mortally wounded, he commits *seppuku* atop Komatsu-*yama*.

By now, the fog has lifted, and the remainder of Mototsugu's vanguard reaches Dōmyōji. Among them is a unit under the command of Susukida Kanesuke, the disgraced commander who due to his nightly carousing failed to save the Toyotomi fort at Bakurōbuchi. Clad in chestnut armor astride a black horse and wielding a cross-shaped lance, he throws himself into the thick of the fight in an effort to restore his reputation. This he does, single-handedly dismounting a dozen enemy warriors on horseback. But when he too falls, the remainder of the vanguard retreats toward Fujiidera, a mile west from Dōmyōji.

It is only at this late juncture that the large rear guard under the command of Sanada Yukimura and Mōri Katsunaga finally catches up with Mototsugu's heavily depleted vanguard. Absorbing the rest of his men into their ranks, they take up positions at Konda, just south of Dōmyōji. There, they also come under fire from Shigenaga's *teppō ashigaru*. But this time the odds are even, as Yukimura has also fielded a large unit of *teppō ashigaru*, who now engage the enemy in a heavy exchange of fire, forcing them back toward Dōmyōji.

After two more hours of heavy fighting, the battle appears to be grinding toward a stalemate when a messenger from the castle arrives with disturbing news: the Toyotomi forces have been dealt a serious blow at Wakae, some seven miles due north from Dōmyōji. The previous evening, ten thousand

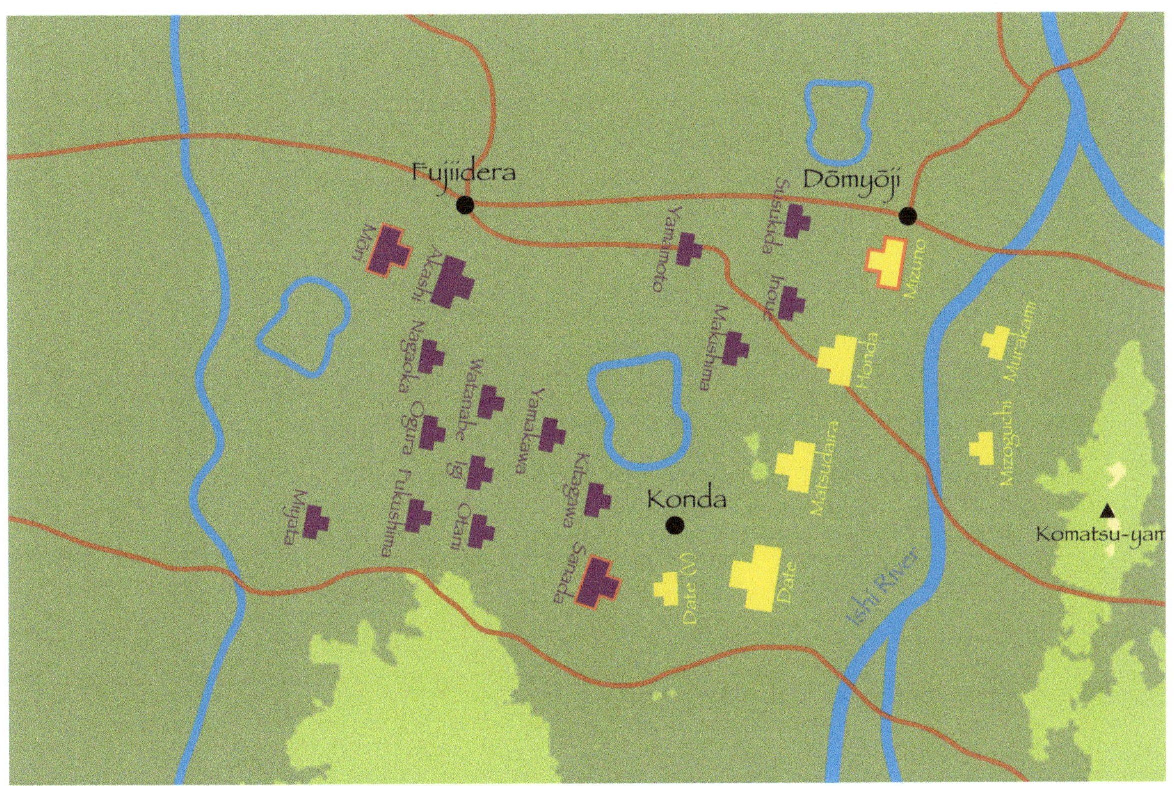

Kimura Shigenari fights his last battle

men under the command of Chōsokabe Morichika and Kimura Shigenari had taken up positions east of the castle to counter the *bakufu* forces advancing along the Higashi Kōya Kaidō. At dawn, Morichika's forces have clashed at Yao with those of Tōdō Takayoshi. The commander of his vanguard has been killed, but he has surprised the enemy's main force by positioning his men behind the raised west bank of the Nagase River. In the battle that follows, three *bakufu* commanders have been killed. Meanwhile, at nearby Wakae, Shigenari has also sought to use the terrain to his advantage by positioning a unit of *teppō ashigaru* on the west bank of the Tamakuji River. It hasn't been enough. Outnumber two to one, they are almost instantly overrun by the forces of Ii Naotaka. For two more hours, Shigenari and his men try to push back the enemy, who have now taken up positions atop the embankment. But when, toward the break of daylight, Shigenari is killed along with two of his commanders, the remainder flees toward the castle. Observing them from Yao, Morichika also orders his men to fall back toward the castle.

The *bakufu* breakthrough at Wakae and Yao presents Yukimura and Katsunaga with a dilemma: continue fending off Mizuno Katsunari's forces at Dōmyōji at the risk of being cut off, or lose their advantage by falling back to fight another day. The die is cast for them by urgent missives from within the castle to withdraw. And thus, as dusk sets in, they reluctantly order their men to withdraw toward Tennōji.

One final time the Toyotomi camp seeks to avert the inevitable. On the morning of 3 June, a glorious summer day, they amass their troops south of the castle, in a slanted line between Ieyasu's former headquarters of Chausu-*yama* and Sasa-*yama*. Its west flank is led by Sanada Yukimura, who has now set up his own headquarters atop Chausu-*yama*. He and his son Nobumasu command a force of more than three thousand men. Behind them, on the grounds of the Isshin Temple, are the forces of Ebara Takatsugu and Hosokawa Okiaki, one of the few members of his clan who have joined the Toyotomi cause. East of the hill, Fukushima Masanori's two sons, Masamoro and Masashige, are in charge of another two thousand. Immediately in front

Sanada Yukimura rallies his forces

of the hill are two thousand more under the shared command of Watanabe Tadasu (who leads Yukimura's mounted guard), Iki Tōkatsu, and Ōtani Yoshiharu. The central thrust of the Toyotomi army, more than six thousand men, is positioned around Tennōji, so named because of the beautiful Shitennō Temple that has graced the area for centuries. They have taken up positions along the southern perimeter of the temple grounds and are under the command of Mōri Katsunaga. Four thousand more warriors, under the overall command of Ōno Harufusa, are stationed farther northeast of Tennōji, around Sasa-*yama*. Behind these three positions are the famed Shichite-*gumi*, the elite guard of the House of Toyotomi. Commanded by Ōno Harunaga, they number some fourteen thousand men and form the Toyotomi rear guard. In all, the Toyotomi camp has fielded some fifty thousand men. It is clear that this battle will decide the outcome of the siege.

This much is borne out, too, by a directive issued to all the commanders in the Toyotomi camp. 'The coming battle,' it predicts, 'will be of the utmost importance as it will decide who will rule the realm.' There are to be no more antics in pursuit of personal glory. Instead, the 'orders issued by central command are to be strictly adhered to.' There are to be no more individual sorties or the kind of attempts at interception that have ended so disastrously over the previous days at Wakae and Yao.

The Toyotomi camp has good reason to keep its men in check. Opposing them is an army almost three times their size. Facing Sanada Yukimura's

Shichite-gumi: Also known as the O-umamawari Shichitō, or the Seven Heads of the Honorable Horse Guard, the Shichite-*gumi* was the elite guard of the House of Toyotomi. First assembled by Hideyoshi during his campaign against the Hōjō at Odawara Castle (at which point it consisted of twelve heads), the Shichite-*gumi* consisted of so-called *kumi-gashira* or 'group leaders,' who enjoyed a stipend between three and ten thousand *koku* each. Though their number fluctuated and was hardly ever seven, they were, like Hideyoshi's Seven Spearmen of Shizugatake, nevertheless referred to as the 'Seven Heads.' Each *kumi-gashira* was in charge of a unit of between a few hundred and a few thousand men.

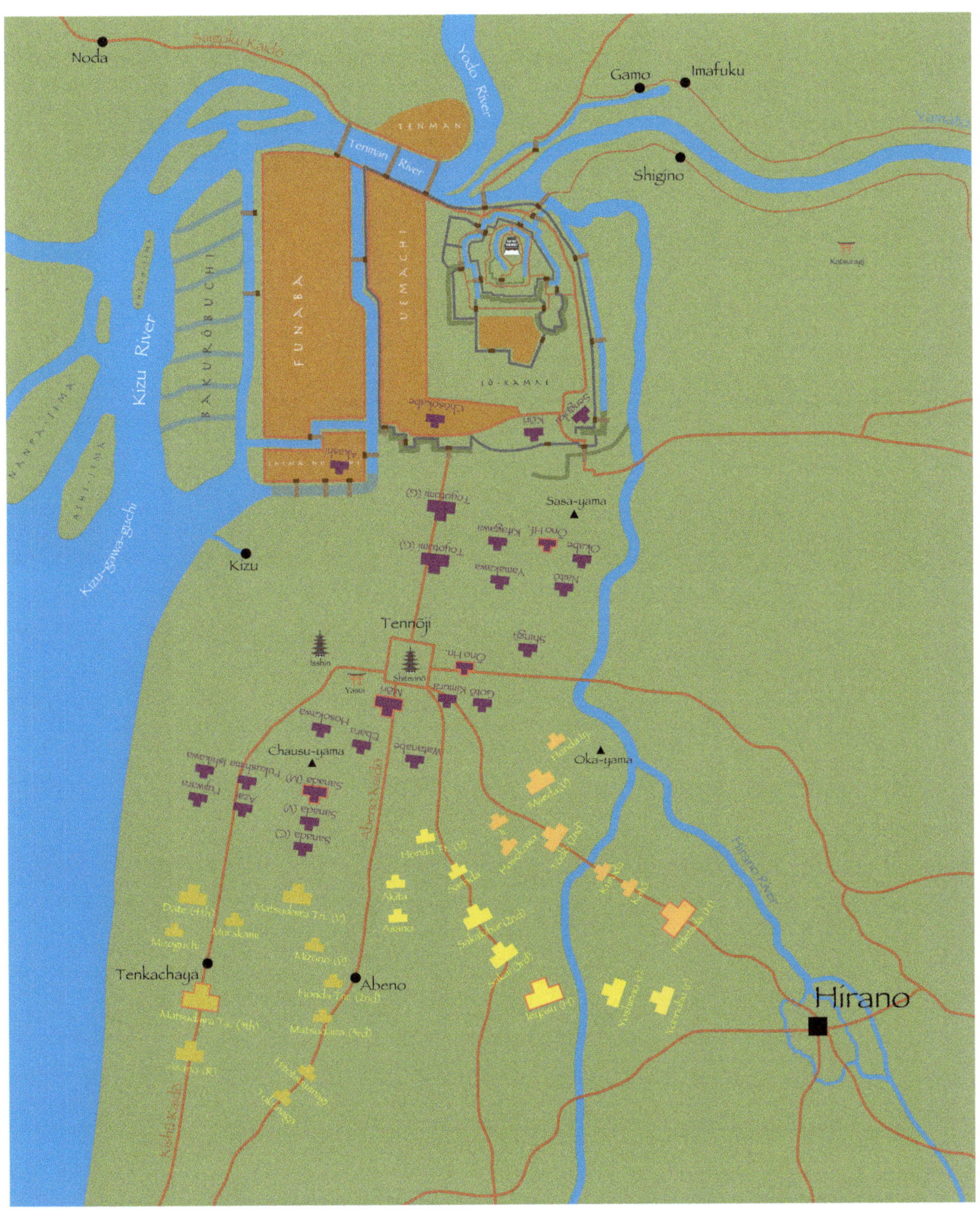
Noda
Yodo River
Gamo
Imafuku
TENMAN
Tenman River
Shigino
UEMACHI
FUNABA
BAKURŌBUCHI
Kizu River
SŌ-KAMAE
Sasa-yama
Kizu
Kizu-gawa-guchi
Tennōji
Chausu-yama
Oka-yama
Abeno Kaidō
Tenkachaya
Abeno
Hirano River
Hirano
Kishū Kaidō

真田幸村
本多忠朝
憤戰圖

Hoda Tadatomo in action at Tennōji

forces from the hamlet of Abeno, just a mile south of Chausu-*yama*, are thirty-five thousand warriors under the command of Ieyasu's grandson, the twenty-year-old Matsudaira Tadanao.

The central Tokugawa thrust toward Tennōji is presented by a vanguard of some 5,000 men under the command of Honda Tadatomo. Immediately behind this vanguard comes a force under the command of Sakakibara Yasukatsu, who controls some 5.000 men, and Sakai Ietsugu. who commands roughly the same number. Behind all these forces, just north of Hirano, sits Ieyasu's *honjin*, his field headquarters with his core army of well over 15.000 men. The rearguard of this huge force is provided by another 15.000 men under the command of his sons, the fourteen-year-old Yoshinao and the thirteen-year-old Yorinobu. The eastern flank of the Tokugawa army, commanded by his son Hidetada, has positioned itself around Oka-*yama*. Its vanguard consists of a force of some 20,000 men under the command of Maeda Toshitsune, Honda Yasutoshi, Honda Yasunori, and Katagiri Katsumoto, the man who played such a vital role during the Battle of Dōmyōji. They are supported by yet more Tokugawa allies, among them Tōdō Takatora, Ii Naotaka, and Honda Tadaoki, who together command some 7,000 men. Hidetada's *honjin* atop Oka-*yama*. His main force consists of well over 20.000 men. The flanks of his forces are under the command of Kuroda Nagamasa and Katō Yoshiaki. In all, the Tokugawa camp has fielded some one hundred and fifty thousand men.

It is already noon when, as if to take pride in this mighty array, Honda Tadatomo, leaves his position and begins to ostentatiously inspect his troops with a small group of mounted warriors. In truth, Tadatomo has another, more important reason to play himself into the picture. He spent much of the Winter Campaign in a drunken stupor and had been relegated to the sidelines. Now, clad in bright crimson armor and a crimson feather gracing his helmet, he is in charge of Matsudaira Tadanao's vanguard, and he is determined to make the most of it.

No sooner has Tadatomo entered no man's land in between the two vast armies than he comes under fire from a unit of some three hundred Negoro *teppō ashigaru* under the command of Watanabe Tadasu. They are positioned at the Kōshin-*dō*, the Shitennō Temple's Hall of the Metal Ape, dedicated to the 57th year of the Chinese calendar. Situated a few hundred yards south of the temple's south gate, it marks the line where the plateau on which the city of Ōsaka stands makes a sudden drop toward the wider Hirano Plain. From there, elevated several yards above the plain, Tadasu's *teppō ashigaru* have a clear bead on anyone who dares to venture into no man's land below.

Startled by the flashes, followed by the reports of the muskets atop the ridge, Tadatomo draws to a sudden halt, and for the briefest of moments, he seems flustered as the hail of lead turns up the dry ground around him. Then, even before the dust has settled, he regains his composure, stands up in his stirrups, raises his right arm, and commands his men to fall upon the enemy. This they do, only to be crushed by a second Toyotomi army group under the command of the Fukushima brothers (Masamoro and Masashige). They are followed on their heels by the forces of Mōri Katsunaga, who splits them into two wings so as to trap Tadatomo's men in a pincer movement. Seeing the enemy fall upon his men, Tadatomo rises once more from his saddle, declaiming in a loud and clear voice his name, title, and feats. Then, uttering his last words by shouting, 'Save him who has erred through liquor!' he directs his horse into the fray, breaking his lance as he falls upon the crushing horde and eventually goes under.

Honda Tadatomo (center) fights his last battle

Honda Tadatomo (1582–1615) was the son of Honda Tadakatsu, a senior retainer of Tokugawa Ieyasu. Tadatomo first saw action in the Battle of Sekigahara at the age of eighteen. Fighting alongside his father, they had clashed with a unit of Satowara *teppō ashigaru* under the command of Shimazu Toyohisa. In the initial volley, his father's prized horse, Mikuniguro, had been shot from underneath him, while Ii Naomasa was severely wounded. It was partly due to Tadatomo's dauntless actions—he took two enemy heads—that the two men survived the battle (Naomasa would succumb to his wounds two years later). When Tadatomo arrived back in camp at the end of the day, his sword was so bent that it would not fit in its scabbard. Ieyasu, too, was impressed, noting that 'Your actions today will earn you a place equal to that of your father.'

It was during Tadatomo's lordship of the Ōtaki domain on the Bōsō Peninsula that, in 1609, a Spanish vessel, the *San Francisco*, was shipwrecked on the nearby coast. Onboard the vessel was Rodrigo de Vivero, who had just completed his tenure as the governor of the Phillippines. De Vivero and the more than 300 other crew members were treated hospitably by Tadatomo, who invited the governor to his castle and arranged for him to visit *shōgun* Tokugawa Hidetada.

In the run-up to the Winter Campaign, Tadatomo was part of Hidetada's vanguard on the latter's departure from Edo, and he was part of Hidetada's guard when he stayed at Nijō Castle for the war council with his father. Tadatomo had initially been stationed near the Katsuragi Shrine, alongside the forces of Uesugi Kagekatsu and Satake Yoshinobu. When, on 26 December, the latter had been ordered to assault the Toyotomi fortifications at Shigino and Imafuku, Tadatomo had been ordered to join their rear guard. Yet Tadatomo, who had been spending the previous night carousing and drinking, failed to show up and it was left to Horio Tadaharu, Niwa Nagashige, and Sakakibara Yasukatsu to do the job.

Once the fortifications had been captured, Tadatomo was ordered to relieve the Satake forces at Imafuku. He set up his headquarters at Nakahama, a hamlet on the north bank of the Yamato River, just west of Imafuku. For the rest of the Winter Campaign, he kept a low profile. His men were attached as an ancillary unit to the forces of Asano Nagashige, who remained stationed at Shigino.

Tadatomo, however, was determined to regain his reputation. On the eve of the Battle of Tennōji, he visited the camp of Hosokawa Tadaoki, asking him to look after his one-year-old son Masakatsu in the event of his death.

Seeing Tadatomo fall, Ogasawara Hidemasa and his son Tadanaga order their men to come to his men's rescue. Leading their men from the front, they attack the Mōri and Fukushima forces, but the moment they clash, their right flank is assaulted by a tactical unit under the command of Kimura Muneaki (who had led the left wing of his nephew Shigenari's forces at Wakae). The twenty-year-old Tadanaga is killed. His forty-six-year-old father, who is mortally wounded, manages to extricate himself from the fight-

The Battle of Tennōji, with Ieyasu's forces on the right and Hideyori's forces on the left

ing. He makes it to the Kyūhō Temple, a stone's throw east of Abeno, where he is visited by one of Ieyasu's men. His last words to Ieyasu are, 'As for Shinano…' He never gets to complete his sentence; wounded in six places, he expired mid-sentence. But Ieyasu knows what he wanted to say. It of course concerns his son, Tadanaga, who should not have been with him in the first place. He had received strict instructions from the *bakufu* to remain at home in Shinano and guard their headquarters of Matsumoto Castle (a duty his fa-

Ieyasu and his guards are caught off-guard

ther had performed during the Winter Campaign). The young warrior had refused. Contravening the *bakufu* instructions, he had come down to Ōsaka to fight alongside his father. Now both men are dead, and all Ieyasu can do is pardon the young warrior for contravening *bakufu* orders.

Ieyasu has little time to mull over the deaths of the two warriors: the battlefield is shifting rapidly. Sanada Yukimura has ordered all the forces positioned around Chausu-*yama*, some ten thousand in all, to attack the forces of Matsudaira Tadanao. The latter, too, has ordered his core of five thousand men to move forward. But just as the two large forces are about to clash, Tadanao's men veer off to the northeast. Like two loggerheads, the two vast forces begin to brush past each other, the Matsudaira force toward the Shitennō Temple's Kōshin-*dō*, the Sanada forces toward Ieyasu's positions near Abeno. All that stands between them are Tadanao's second and third divisions. The former is made up of four units under the command of Sakakibara Yasukatsu, who had helped save the day at Wakae; the latter is made up of five units under the command Sakai Ietsugu. Both of them offer fierce resistance but, outnumbered two to one, their formations eventually collapse under the overwhelming pressure.

Ieyasu and his men are utterly caught off-guard: Tadanao's vanguard has been destroyed, his main army has veered off toward the Shitennō-*ji*'s Kōshindō, and his second and third divisions have crumbled. It leaves Ieyasu's positions totally exposed to the huge force that is rapidly moving toward them.

It is at this critical moment that the rumor begins to spread among the Tokugawa ranks that Asano Nagaakira, the lord of Wakayama Castle, who is in command of their rear guard, has turned against them and is now threatening to also attack them from the rear. It is just a rumor: Nagaakira is still firmly on their side, waiting in the wings along the Kishū Kaidō near Anryū (some three miles south of Tenkachaya). Yet the rumor sticks and spreads like wildfire among the nervous Tokugawa ranks.

Sensing the panic among Ieyasu's men, Yukimura splits his men three units, which roll over the Tokugawa ranks in devastating waves that threaten to drown them. Up to three times, they clash with Ieyasu's disoriented men, driving deep into their lines. And each time they are led by a fearless Yukimura. At one stage, they get within yards of Ieyasu's camp, causing a

徳川大君家康公
水野帯刀
大久保彦左エ門

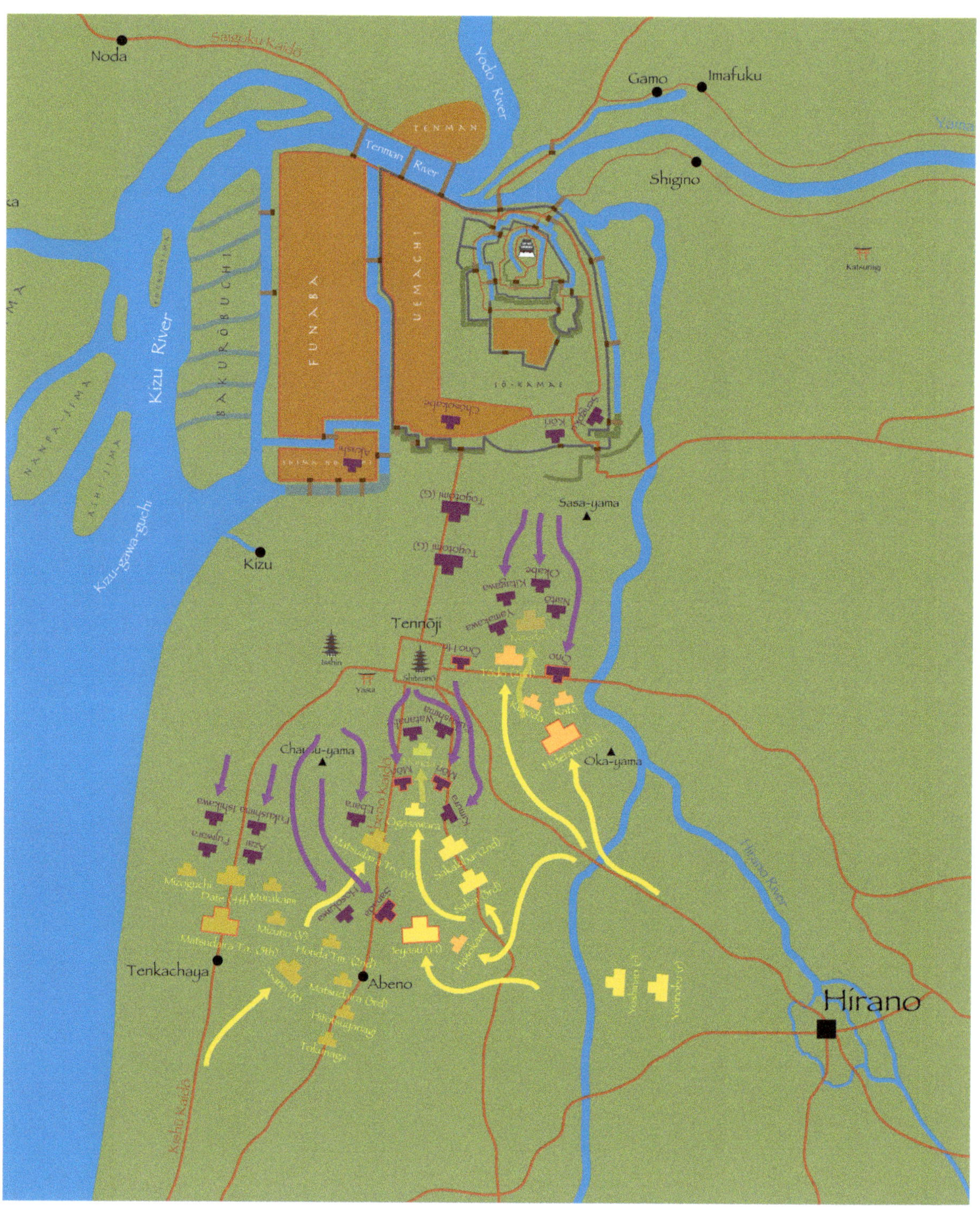
Noda
Yodo River
Gamo
Imafuku
TENMAN
Tenman River
Shigino
UEMACHI
FUNABA
BAKURŌBUCHI
Kizu River
Kizu-gawa-guchi
Kizu
Sasa-yama
Tennōji
Oka-yama
Tenkachaya
Abeno
Hirano
Hirano River

Sanada Yukimura and his forces overrun Ieyasu's ranks

number of his bannermen to abandon their positions and flee southward along toward Kōya Kaidō. Then the hata-*bugyō*, the man holding the Tokugawa banner at the rear of Ieyasu's camp, stumbles and falls, and with him so does the Tokugawa banner. It is only the second time since Ieyasu's humiliating defeat at Mikatagahara against the great Takeda Shingen that his banner touches the soil. With his mind flashing back to that traumatic moment in his life, the *Tenka-dono*, too, loses his composure. Drawing his horse to the side of the road, he begins to stammer as if to himself, contemplating *seppuku*, according to some.

Meanwhile, over at Oka-*yama*, things are faring no better for Ieyasu's son. Observing the opening of hostilities over at Tennōji from atop the hill, Hidetada has ordered his troops to advance toward the castle. Some fifteen thousand of Maeda Toshitsune's men begin to move toward Sasa-*yama* where they come under intense fire from a unit of *teppō ashigaru* under the command of Ōno Harufusa. When Toshitsune's vanguard begins to collapse, reinforcements under the command of Ii Naotaka and Tōdō Takatora come to their rescue but they, too, fail to keep formation. Seizing the moment, Harufusa orders his men to overrun them and attack the camp of Hidetada atop Oka-*yama*, just a mile toward the south. In this, they almost succeed when they reach the foot

The Yasui Shrine, the place where Sanada Yukimura met his end

of the hill and clash with Hidetada's bannermen under the command of Doi Toshikatsu. These, too, threaten to give way, at which point the assailants begin to scorn Toshikatsu aloud. Enraged, Hidetada grabs a lance from one of his bannermen and makes ready to throw himself into the fight, when Honda Masanobu grabs the reins of his horse and bids him to stop and look toward Tennōji. Following Masanobu's gaze, the young *shōgun*'s face lights up—the tide is turning; Ieyasu's men have recovered from the blows, fallen back into formation, and are now unmistakably advancing northward along the Kōya Kaidō toward Tennōji. A mile farther eastward, the forces of Matsudaira Tadaaki and Asano Nagakira are doing the same along the Kishū Kaidō.

Only one thing has saved the day for Ieyasu and Hidetada: superiority in numbers. Despite the withering assaults, their men still outnumber the enemy by three to one. Moreover, they may have lost thousands—so have the Toyotomi, and with just fifty thousand men to start with, it is the Toyotomi who are unable to sustain the attrition.

Their plight is embodied by the last moments of Sanada Yukimura, the hero of Ōsaka Castle's defense. Having spent himself in the three withering but fruitless sorties into the Tokugawa ranks, the valiant warrior, gravely wounded in several places, withdraws to the grounds of the Yasui shrine, just north of Chausu-*yama*. There, he dismounts and seeks solace in the shadow of a large pine tree to nurse his wounds. It is at this point that Nishio Munetsugu, a *kumi-gashira* in Matsudaira Tadanao's unit of *teppō ashigaru*, who is passing through the grounds in the general thrust toward the castle, spots the wounded Yukimura leaning against the tree and is stopped in his tracks. Seeing the warrior, the latter murmurs, 'I am Sanada Yukimura, an adversary no doubt quite worthy of you, but I am too exhausted to fight any longer. Come, take my head and make it your trophy!' Then, in a final effort, he removes his helmet and nods to the warrior with an air of resignation as the latter raises his sword and cuts off his head.

It is as if, with Yukimura's life, all resistance among the Toyotomi troops ebbs away. Overwhelmed by the enemy's superiority in numbers, they gradually retreat toward the castle. By roughly five o'clock in the afternoon, the hour of the Monkey, all the Toyotomi troops have withdrawn behind the stronghold's imposing walls.

浪花百景
安居天神社
彫工板定
石和板
芳雪画

It is now that the superiority in equipment also begins to play into the hands of the Tokugawa forces. Only a few days earlier, more and heavier cannon have arrived: twelve twenty-five-pounders from Holland and another four eighteen-pound culverins from England. They are manned by special squads of gunners who have been trained by Dutch and English mercenaries and are able to hit their target with remarkable precision.

With whole sections of the castle's southern moats still filled in and their walls pounded by the newly arrived cannon, it is only a matter of hours before the first breaches are made in the stronghold's southern defenses. The first Tokugawa troops to enter the breach are those of Matsudaira Tadanao and Mizuno Katsunari. Having overrun the enemy positions at Chausu-*yama*, they break through the Hatchōme Gate in the castle's south wall and pour into the wide area surrounding the castle's outer baileys. From there, they work their way clockwise around the filled-in second moat toward the Ikutama-*guchi*'s Ōte-*mon*, the main gate that gives access to the castle's second bailey. Before long, the main gate, too, is breached and the first troops enter the second bailey. There, the remainder of Hideyori's loyal Shichite-*gumi* puts up a valiant last struggle, but by six o'clock, the hour of the Rooster, they have all perished and the assailants finally reach the Sakura-*mon*, the main gate giving access to the stronghold's inner citadel. It is men from Mizuno Katsunari's troops, among them the famed swordsman Miyamoto Musashi, who manage to climb the gate and erect the Mizuno banner.

One more factor plays into the Tokugawa hands at this point: they have another mole inside the castle. His name is Ōsumi Yozaemon, and he is in charge of the castle's large kitchen, which is one among the many buildings that make up the Oku-*goten*, Hideyori's private quarters at the foot of the castle's main keep. Hearing that the enemy has reached the Sakura-*mon*, he orders his personnel to set fire to the kitchen. The rainy season has not yet begun and a stiff western breeze causes the flames to jump from one building to the next until they reach the foot of the five-story main keep.

It is perhaps out of reverence for the Toyotomi heir that, even while the main keep is ablaze, the Tokugawa troops refrain from entering the castle's inner citadel. Instead, negotiations commence between the Tokugawa camp and those still holed up inside.

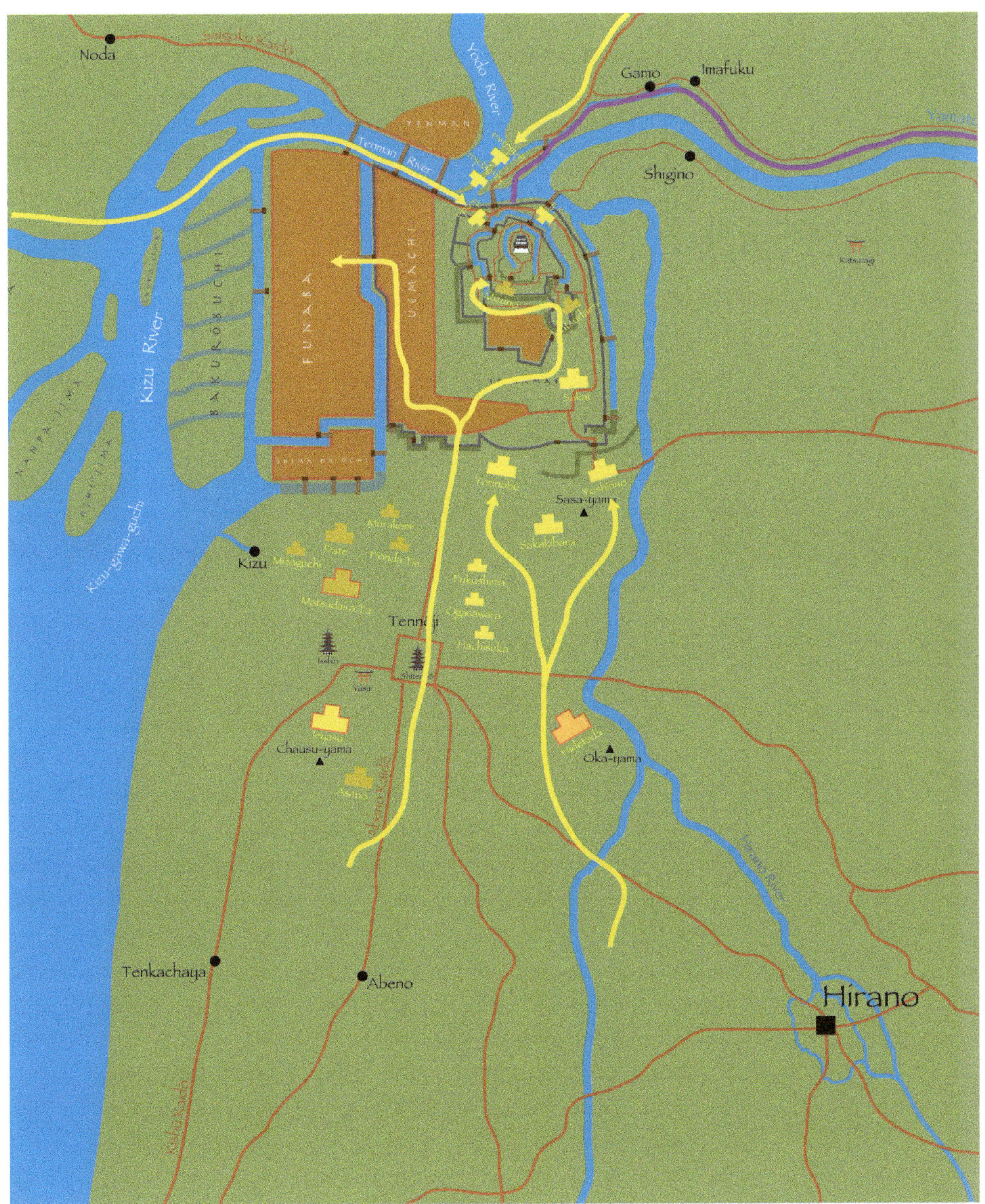
Noda
Saigoku Kaido
Yodo River
Gamo
Imafuku
Shigino
Katsuragi
TENMAN
Tenman River
FUNABA
UEMACHI
BAKUROBUCHI
Kizu River
NANBA-JIMA
ASHI-JIMA
Kizu-gawa-guchi
Kizu
Mizoguchi
Date
Murakami
Honda Tm.
Matsudaira Ta.
Fukushima
Ogasawara
Hachisuka
Sakakibara
Sasa-yama
Tennoji
Chausu-yama
Ieyasu
Asano
Oka-yama
Abeno Kaido
Hirano River
Tenkachaya
Abeno
Hirano
Kishu Kaido

The beautiful Sen-*hime*, the last but vain hope of the Toyotomi camp

By now, most of the structures amid the inner citadel have gone up in flames. To escape them, the few survivors retreat to the Tsukimi-*yagura*, the turret at the northwest corner of the Oku-*goten* compound. From there, they move down into the Yamazato-*kuruwa*, a small, separate bailey on the north side of the inner citadel. There, at the foot of the burning keep, in a small cluster of buildings that together form the tea retreat built by his father, Hideyori, his mother, and his womenfolk, anxiously await the fate that lies in store for them. With them are a few dozen of their most loyal retainers. Chief among them are Mōri Katsunaga and Ōno Harunaga. It is on the initiative of Harunaga—who is mortally wounded himself—that a messenger by the name of Yonekura Kenuemon is sent across the nearby Rōka Bridge. He carries with him a plea in which Harunaga, Katsunaga, and all the other surviving retainers offer their lives in exchange for the lives of the young heir, his mother, and his womenfolk. To add force to their plea and mollify the *shōgun*, they send along his daughter, the beautiful Sen-*hime*. She is accompanied by her chief ladies-in-waiting and a small escort of Toyotomi stalwarts. The small party, blood-stained and covered in ashes, is initially received by men under the command of Sakazaki Naomori. He immediately sends them on with an escort of his own to Ieyasu, who has meanwhile set up camp for the night at his former headquarters atop Chausu-*yama*.

Still unable to bring the death of Hideyoshi's heir down on himself, Ieyasu leaves the fate of Hideyori and the other survivors in the hands of his son. The sly old fox knows what he is doing. The more cruelly inclined Hideyori, is unmoved. Far from it: he is outraged that his daughter has had the temerity to escape; she should have remained within the castle and ended her life alongside her husband. He nevertheless lets her live but condemns all those who remain within the castle to death. That cruel and unforgiving message is delivered in likewise fashion at the first light of day early next morning, when a salvo from Ii Naotaka's *teppō ashigaru* rips through the thin walls of the buildings amid the Yamazato-*kuruwa*.

Hidetada's message is understood by all those within the Yamazato-*kuruwa*. The first to depart this world is the young Hideyori, who appoints Mōri Katsunaga as his *kaishaku* and cuts open his belly. He is immediately followed by his mother, Yodo-*dono*, who according to tradition, slits her throat and is de-

一魁斎芳年筆
大橋

The **Yamazato**-*kuruwa* lay in the crescent-shaped northern section of the egg-shaped island that formed the inner citadel of Hideyoshi's Ōsaka Castle. It was set off from the rest of the inner citadel in that it lay outside the thick castle wall that encircled the central area (the Tsume no Maru), which housed the Oku-*goten* and the main keep. The Yamazato-*kuruwa* did not fill the entire crescent. A third of its area, situated on the west side and known as the Ashida-*kuruwa*, housed the accommodations of the castle guards.

The buildings amid the Yamazato-*kuruwa* were built by Hideyoshi as a retreat where he and his illustrious guest could participate in tea ceremonies conducted by the likes of Sen no Rikyū and Tsuda Sōgyū. It was the place to which he retreated to calm his nerves following the disastrous reception of the Ming embassy, and It was the place to which his wife withdrew in early spring to watch the blossoming cherry trees in the Yamazato-*kuruwa*'s beautiful garden.

Some of the buildings were used during the Winter and Summer campaigns to coin the emergency gold bullion by which the vast numbers of *rōnin* were paid).

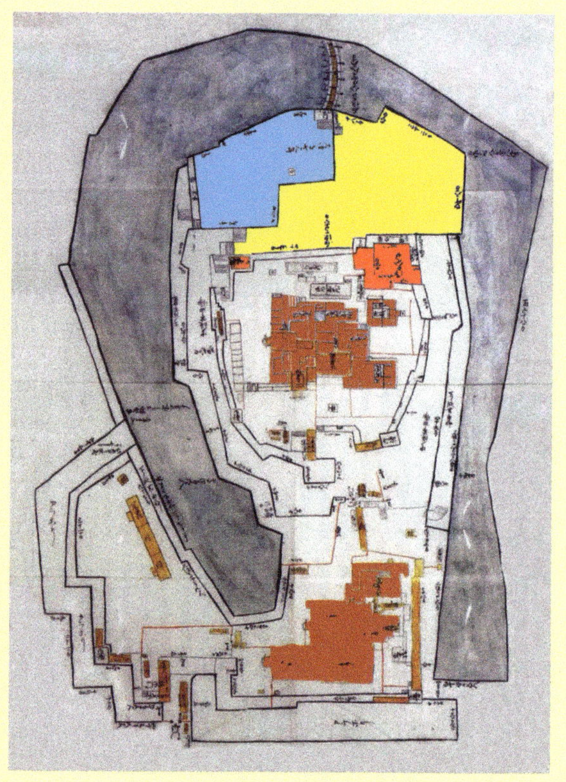

Ōsaka Castle's inner citadel. The two goten *are marked in brown, the main keep and Tsukimi-yagura in red, the Yamazato-*kuruwa *in yellow, and the Ashida-*kuruwa *is marked in blue.*

capitated by Ōno Harunaga. Thirty-three survivors in all end their lives that morning, at the hour of the Dragon on 4 June 1615. Among them are the two *kaishaku*, Mōri Katsunaga and Ōno Harunaga, their sons, and some two dozen loyal retainers. The wretched party also includes six of Yodo-*dono* and Sen-*hime*'s ladies in waiting. One of them is Ōkurakyō no Tsubone, a woman who, along with Yodo-*dono* (whose wetnurse she had been), wielded great influence in the Toyotomi clan. It was she who, that previous summer, had gone up to Sunpu Castle to try and resolve Katagiri Katsumoto's conflict with Ieyasu over the inscription on the temple bell of the Hōkō Temple.

GLOSSARY

ashigaru: Foot soldier.
bakufu: Military, lit. 'tent,' government.
bugyō: Magistrate.
buke yashiki: Samurai mansion.
cha nu yū: The art of making and drinking tea.
daimyō: Feudal lord.
demaru: Barbican.
funakura: Boat house.
Go-Bugyō: Council of (five) Commissioners.
Go-Tairō: Council of (five) Regents.
goten: Castle palace.
hirayamajō: A castle partly built atop a hill or mountain and partly on the surrounding plane.
honjin: A commander's filed headquarters.
honjō: The main castle at the center of a network of strongholds.
hori-kiri: A moat cut across the crest of a hill or mountain.
hoshi-goroshi: Siege tactic whereby a castle is cut off from its supplies.
hyōjō: A lord's council with his chief retainers.
ichiban-nori: The first warrior to breach a castle's defenses.
jinjō: Makeshift fortress.

kaishaku:	The assistant who cuts off someone's head during seppuku.
kinzō:	Storehouse the place where a lord kept his bullion.
kofun:	Ancient burial mound.
koku:	Measure, equal to about 5 bushels.
kumi-gashira:	Group leader.
kuruwa:	Bailey.
mizu-zeme:	Siege tactic whereby a castle is flooded.
naginata:	Lance.
nō:	Classical Japanese dance-drama.
rōnin:	Masterless *samurai*.
seppuku:	Ritual suicide in which a person plunged his dagger into his lower abdomen.
shijō:	Satellite castle.
shoshidai:	The *shōgun*'s deputy in Kyoto.
shugo:	Provincial governor.
shōgun:	Hereditary military governor during Japan's fuedal era.
shōji-bori:	Lit 'paper screen moat.' A moat in which the floor of the moat was covered by a checkered pattern of ridges.
soto-kamae:	Outer defensive layer of a castle.
sōhei:	Warrior monk(s).
taiko:	Drum.
Taikō-sama:	Honorary name specifically used for Toyotomi Hideyoshi.
tamon-yagura:	An elongated structures or nagaya that covers a stretch of a stronghold's earthen rampart or stone wall.
Tenka-dono:	Honorary name specifically used for Tokugawa Ieyasu.
tenshū:	Main keep of a castle.
teppō ashigaru:	Foot soldiers armed with muskets.
teppō bugyō:	Magistrate of muskets.
toride:	Fortification.
umadashi:	Horse break-out.
umetate bugyō:	Magistrate in charge of filling in moats.
yamashiro:	Mountain stronghold.
yari:	Lance.
ōzuchu:	Handheld and ground-placed mortar.

INDEX

U

W

Y

Z

IN THE SAME SERIES

SAMURAI BATTLES

THE LONG ROAD TO UNIFICATION

WILLIAM DE LANGE

TOYO PRess publishes books that contribute to a deeper understanding of Asian cultures. Book and cover design: Chōkei Studios. Printing and binding: IngramSpark. The typefaces are Purloin, Futurist, and Marcellus.

www.ingramcontent.com/pod-product-compliance
Ingram Content Group UK Ltd.
Pitfield, Milton Keynes, MK11 3LW, UK
UKHW061952290726
14090UKWH00021B/1189